An attorney in Dublin died exceedingly poor. A shilling subscription was requested to pay his funeral expenses.

Most of the lawyers and barristers subscribed, and one of them applied to Judge McClannahan, expressing his hope that his lordship would also subscribe his shilling.

"Only a shilling," said the judge, "only a shilling to bury an attorney? Here is a Guinea! Go bury twenty of them!"

**THE OFFICIAL LAWYERS JOKE BOOK**

# THE
# OFFICIAL
# LAWYERS
# JOKEBOOK

## LARRY WILDE

### Illustrations by Ron Wing

BANTAM BOOKS

TORONTO · NEW YORK · LONDON · SYDNEY

THE OFFICIAL LAWYERS JOKE BOOK

*A Bantam Book/February 1982*

*Drawings by Ron Wing.*

ISBN   0-553-20111-5

*Published simultaneously in the United States and Canada*

PRINTED IN THE UNITED STATES OF AMERICA

0  9  8  7  6  5  4  3  2  1

*The first thing we do,*
*let's kill all the lawyers.*
WILLIAM SHAKESPEARE
*King Henry VI*, Act III

## DEDICATED TO:

*Sam Perlmutter, my friend,
my golf partner, my lawyer,
and Montebello's noblest macho
mirth maker.*

# *CONTENTS*

## Introduction

*Woe unto you, Lawyers!*
Luke 11:52

As objects of humor, lawyers follow right in the footsteps of the politicians and doctors. We fight back against the legal practitioners the only way we can—with laughter. (You wouldn't want to take them into court, would you?)

Cracking jokes about people you can't cope with is a time-honored pastime for Americans. Will Rogers, Mark Twain, Josh Billings, and Artemus Ward made a handsome living out of doing just that. Their caustic comments on political life made many a politician wince and wish he had a hole to crawl into. But the lawyers, ah, they have been fodder for the comedic cannon since the English barristers first donned their wigs and gowns.

The following example is documented in a collection of wit and humor from 1899. Its original source can be traced as far back as the 1700s:

*An attorney in Dublin died exceedingly poor. A shilling subscription was requested to pay his funeral expenses.*

*Most of the lawyers and barristers subscribed, and one of them applied to Judge McClannahan, expressing his hope that his lordship would also subscribe his shilling.*

*"Only a shilling," said the judge. "Only a shilling to bury an attorney? Here is a guinea! Go bury twenty of them!"*

Doctors must deal every day with colds, coughs, and kidney problems; politicians have to cope with pollution, inflation, and taxes. But the lawyers get to do business with folks involved in prostitution, murder, and rape—all the fun things.

Consider that these counselors-at-law must rub elbows with swindlers, robbers, bigamists, connivers, crooks, convicts, hookers, pimps, and drug pushers—the cream of society. Not exactly a life of serenity, and the attorney has always had to face the sneers and ridicule of his fellow man, to boot.

There was no better practitioner of humor to illustrate a point than Abraham Lincoln. The following represents his tongue-in-cheek view of the legal profession:

*Lincoln was involved in a case to be heard in the local courthouse and so he entered the town tavern the evening before. When Abe reached the inn, the huge fireplace in the sitting room was surrounded by all the other lawyers interested in the case.*

*"Really cold out, eh?" asked the innkeeper.*

*"Colder than hell," answered Lincoln.*

*"You've been there, too, Mr. Lincoln?" asked a bystander.*

*"Oh, yes." Abe smiled. "And it's just as it is here. All the lawyers are nearest the fire."*

The Watergate affair produced evidence that some of our biggest lawyers were closest to the fire. The profession of Richard Nixon, John Mitchell, John Ehrlichman et al. prompted John Dean's oft-quoted question: "How in God's name could so many lawyers get involved in something like this?"

Humorist Art Buchwald hit the nail on the head when he wrote:

*It isn't the bad lawyers who are screwing up the justice system in this country— it's the good lawyers . . . if you have two competent lawyers on opposite sides, a trial that should take three days, could easily last six months.*

This attitude toward members of the bar appears to be prevalent especially among those unfortunate persons having any legal entanglement. And it's not just here on earth, either:

*One day the gate between heaven and hell broke down. St. Peter called out to the devil, ''Hey, Satan, it's your turn to fix it.''*

*''Sorry,'' said the devil. ''My men are too busy shoveling coal. We can't worry about a mere gate.''*

*''All right,'' declared St. Peter, ''I'll have to sue you for breaking our agreement.''*

*''Go ahead!'' snapped Satan. ''Where are you gonna get a lawyer?''*

Here's a chance to chuckle over some choice lawyer lampooning. This compendium covers every comic aspect of the legal profession, including the enormous contributions made by our law enforcement agencies.

According to the American Bar Association, the number of lawyers in America is growing far faster than the population. Today, in the United States, there is one lawyer for every 470 persons. It appears that sooner or later we must all be involved in some form of litigation.

The only thing is that with *The Lawyers Joke Book* in hand, we can now, at least, laugh all the way to the courtroom.

LARRY WILDE

*Los Angeles, 1981*

## *Legal Levity*

Gates and Nugent were chatting about their teenagers.

"And what's your boy going to do for a living?" asked Gates.

"I'm gonna let him be a lawyer," said Nugent. "He's always putting his nose into other people's business, so he might just as well get paid for his time."

\* \* \*

## WILL

*A dead give-away*

Mrs. Kingsley, a wealthy old lady, sent for Peale to make out her will.

The lawyer was gentle and sympathetic. "Now don't you worry about this," he said to the ailing dowager. "Just leave it all to me."

"I might as well." The old woman sighed. "You'll get it, anyway."

* * *

Nadall had an important trial coming up, so he went to the finest tailor in Chicago and ordered a custom-made suit. When he arrived for the final fitting, Nadall was delighted at the wonderful cut, the marvelous texture of the cloth, and the magnificent styling. But when he went to put his money into the pockets, Nadall found there weren't any.

"But why no pockets?" he protested to the tailor.

"You don't need 'em," answered the tailor. "Who ever heard of a lawyer with his hands in his own pockets?"

* * *

Silverstein had been arrested for speeding, passing a red light, going through a stop sign, and driving without a license. He hired his nephew, just graduated from law school, and demanded a trial by jury.

"But you can't win in court," said his friend Levine.

"I know," said Silverstein, "but this is my nephew's first case, and I want him to lose so he'll get an honest job."

\* \* \*

Chapman completed his medical examination and the doctor said to him, "I'm sorry to tell you this but your heart is in bad shape. You'll need a transplant. It's a serious operation and quite expensive."

"How much?" asked Chapman.

"Well, I've got a heart in the freezer now of a man who was thirty-five years old," said the surgeon. "He exercised moderately, never ate fried foods, it's a fairly good organ. It'll cost you $100,000."

"Okay," said Chapman, "but I don't buy a heart very often. Do you have anything better?"

"You can have the heart of a twenty year old Decathlon winner. He never smoked or drank, he was in perfect physical condition. That one costs $250,000."

"Look, doc, we're talking about my life, is there anything better? What's the best you've got?"

"If you really want to go first class, the very best, we happen to have here the heart of a man who was 65 years old. He drank and smoked to excess. Never exercised. Let himself get flabby. Had high cholesterol. It's $1,000,000."

"But why so much for that one?" asked Chapman.

"This is the heart of an attorney and it has never been used."

\* \* \*

Bill Bluestein, California's consummate counselor-at-law, says that the difference between making love to a girl and making love to a woman can be as much as twenty years in some states.

\* \* \*

Marjorie rushed into the house and told her mom that since her boy friend had just passed his bar exams, they wanted to get married.

"Don't you think it'd be a good idea for him to practice for a year first?" asked the woman.

"But, mother," she replied, "we have been practicing!"

\* \* \*

Hamner the advertising exec began shouting at his pretty secretary.

"We may have been to bed a few times together, but who said you could be late for work?"

"My lawyer," said the girl.

\* \* \*

Knox and Watkins rode on the Long Island commuter train. One morning, Knox said, "Hey, you're a lawyer. What's the fine for making a librarian ten days overdue?"

\* \* \*

Carlson finished up his last case, and the firm gave him two weeks for a honeymoon. As he and his new bride got into the elevator at their honeymoon hotel, the operator, a dynamite redhead, smiled at Carlson. She looked at him and said, "Hello, darling."

There was an icy silence until the newlyweds reached their room. Then the bride roared, "Who was that girl?"

"Look, honey," said the lawyer, "don't get excited. I'm going to have enough trouble explaining you to her."

## JOVIAL JUSTICE

The lawyer fell on a banana skin,
　　His torn clothes made him feel
That, as the legal words explain—
　　His suit was lost on a peel.

\* \* \*

While vacationing in a small North Carolina town, attorney Barrett stopped to chat with Combs, an old-timer sitting in front of the courthouse. ''I was wondering,'' said Barrett, ''did you ever have any famous hangings hereabouts?''

''Oh, fella named Dimsdale was sentenced to be hung for a murder he claimed he didn't do,'' answered Combs. ''They had the rope 'round his neck when somethin' went wrong with the trap. It couldn't be sprung. So they took Dimsdale back to his cell until repairs could be made.

''While waitin', the supreme court granted Dimsdale a new trial, and the hangin' was postponed. Then the real murderer was caught, confessed, and Dimsdale was freed. He got married, settled down, and had sixteen kids.''

''But he never did get hung,'' said Barrett.

''You joshin'?'' wisecracked the old-timer. ''With sixteen kids, I'd say he was well hung!''

# BAR ASSOCIATION'S THEME SONG

*Sweet Sue*

* * *

Halfway up a pine-tree-covered Alpine mountainside, there stood a tiny village. Nearby, in an abbey, lived a group of friars who terrorized the villagers. The friars, in order to enrich their coffers, sold flowers at gun point to the townspeople.

Fed up with being forced against their will to buy the flowers, the people held a meeting. "There is only one thing to do," said the mayor. "We must get someone who can stop the friars from bothering us."

"I believe I have the answer," said one of the townsmen. "My cousin Hugh is a big Philadelphia lawyer. He can do anything."

They sent all the way to Pennsylvania for Hugh, and it worked out just as they wished. He stopped the villagers from being harassed. In appreciation of his enormous accomplishment, the townfolks put up a hand-carved notice for visitors to see as they entered the town:

*Hugh, and only Hugh, can*
*stamp out florist friars.*

Doovid Barskin, the lovable television talent rep, tells this little teaser:

Nolan was leaving the cemetery after planting flowers on his wife's grave. Suddenly, he stopped before a tombstone that read:

*Here lies a lawyer,*
*and an honest man.*

"How do you like that?" he murmured. "Times are so bad, they're putting them two in a grave!"

HERE LIES A LAWYER AND AN HONEST MAN

\* \* \*

At a recent psychologists' convention, the chairman made this observation in his keynote address:

"Kids who never come when they are called probably will grow up to be doctors. Kids who show up without being called probably will grow up to be lawyers."

\* \* \*

## NEWSPAPER AD

*Help Wanted: Busy lawyer seeks alert young woman to act as deceptionist.*

\* \* \*

Folcroft had been working on a case out of town for several weeks. He returned home one night and discovered his wife in bed with another man.

"What is the meaning of this?" he demanded. "Who is this fellow?"

"That's a fair question, counselor," said the wife, rolling over. "What *is* your name?"

\* \* \*

When a student first enters law school, he is provided with a huge book containing the subjects to study. The table of contents reads like this:

\* \* \*

Steve Gordon, the rollicking Westwood real estate investor, gets roars with this roaster:

Two Madison Avenue ad execs, Drayton and Wade, were discussing the pros and cons of America's legal system.

"You can't really count on the law, can you?" stated Drayton.

"It's incredible!" answered Wade. "My wife was suing me for divorce. She said I was sterile. I got a lawyer to represent me. At the same time, our housekeeper went down to the courthouse and signed a paper charging me with being the father of her baby. I had to get another lawyer. And would you believe? *I lost both cases.*"

\* \* \*

11

Mrs. Greenberg and Mrs. Friedman, two grandmothers, sat poolside at Grossinger's and chatted about their children.

"My son is a lawyer!" bragged Mrs. Greenberg.

"Yeah?" said Mrs. Friedman. "So how's he doin'?"

"My son is so brilliant he could look at a contract and immediately tell you whether it's oral or written."

\* \* \*

Did you hear about the process server in Fort Wayne who's getting altogether too cocky to suit his cronies?

They don't like the way he's been putting on the writs.

\* \* \*

Air Force Col. Bill Dick delights cronies at the officer's club with this dandy:

Cecile and Sonia were having cocktails. "Whatever is the matter?" asked Cecile. "You're absolutely falling apart?"

"I can't help it," sobbed Sonia. "Harold got so excited about reincarnation that he went to a lawyer and changed his will. He's leaving everything to himself."

\* \* \*

# BUMPER STICKER

*Lawyers do it in their briefs.*

\* \* \*

Mrs. Pearson was sitting in a fashionable shoe store trying on some new pumps. Suddenly, she noticed the salesman who had been waiting on her, staring up her dress. "My God!" she exclaimed, "what are you doing?"

"That sure is pretty," said the wide-eyed shoe seller. "I'd like to get some ice cream, shove it up there, and eat!"

The woman threw a box of shoes at the man and stormed out of the shop. She hailed a cab and rushed downtown to her husband's law office. Mrs. Pearson ran past the receptionist, waved off his secretary, and barged into Mr. Pearson's office.

"I have never been so insulted in my life," she exclaimed. "I want you to sue that store for every cent they've got."

"What happened?"

Mrs. Pearson explained in detail what had taken place. When she finished, she shouted, "Never mind suing! I want you to go down there and beat the hell out of that bastard!"

"Well, honey," said the lawyer, "anybody who can eat that much ice cream, I'm not gonna pick on!"

\* \* \*

Jackie Gayle, the popular Las Vegas funny man, got screams with this line at a Slappy White Friars' Roast:

"I've got a great lawyer. He got Ray Charles a driver's license."

\* \* \*

Did you hear about the Ozark hillbilly who passed away and left his estate in trust for his grieving wife?

She can't touch it till she's thirteen.

\* \* \*

Babbington and Raford, two Kentuckians, were having a friendly sip of Jack Daniels.

"I know you need a lawyer, and I'd like to recommend my boy," said Babbington.

"But your son has never won a case," said Raford.

"I know. But he can lose for you cheaper than any other lawyer in Louisville!"

\* \* \*

"My wife should've been a lawyer."

"Why's that?"

"Every time we have an argument and she feels she's losing, she takes it to a higher court—her mother."

\* \* \*

Arthur Davis, Florida's foremost legal adviser, fills in friends with this howler:

O'Shaughnessy needed a lawyer to represent him in a case he had pending. In the yellow pages, he spotted a firm called "Murphy, Cavanaugh, O'Rourke, and Bernstein."

He went in and asked to see Murphy. O'Shaughnessy was shown to his office, and the two men had a long discussion about the case. Finally, O'Shaughnessy stood up and said, "Murphy, before I give you the case, there is one thing I'd like to know. How did Bernstein get into this firm?"

"Oh," said Murphy, "he represents the finance company. That's the only way we could keep the furniture."

\* \* \*

Coldwell knew that his wife was being unfaithful, so he hired a private eye to tail her. A week later, the investigator reported that Mrs. Coldwell was sleeping with Watkins, a well-known lawyer.

Coldwell decided to handle the situation in a businesslike manner. He called in his secretary and dictated this letter:

*Sir:*

*For some time now you have been carrying on an affair with my wife. So that we can settle this matter intelligently, please*

16

*see me in my office Monday morning at eleven A.M. sharp.*

The lawyer called in his own secretary and sent this reply:

*Dear Sir:*

*Received your circular letter today. You are advised that I will attend the scheduled conference on time.*

\* \* \*

## AMERICA

*A country in which they lock up juries and let defendants loose*

\* \* \*

Patrick Wood, the clever California Realtors attorney, told this corker at a real estate seminar:

A cannibal walked into the neighborhood butcher store and was trying to make up his mind on what to buy for dinner. He saw a sign that read: Realtors' Brains, $5 a pound. Then another that said: Lawyers' Brains, $150 a pound.

"Say, mister," asked the cannibal, "why are lawyers' brains so expensive?"

"Well," said the butcher, "do you know how many attorneys we have to kill to get a pound of brains?"

\* \* \*

\* \* \*

One morning, Mrs. Komorowski walked into the surrogate's office and said, "Are you the judge of reprobate?"

"I am the probate judge."

"Well, I guess this is the right place," said the Polish woman. "My husband died intesticled and left no infidels."

"Lady," said the judge, "the word is intestate, and I assume you also mean codicil."

"I guess so, judge. I just want to be the executioner."

\* \* \*

Bill Peterson, the prominent Chicago attorney, pleases pals with this playful pleasantry:

An old-time Illinois political leader was approached by a young Rockford lawyer who was eager to get to the state capital. The old politico was doubtful of the attorney's integrity.

"Counselor, if you promise me solemnly that you will not steal when you get to Springfield," said the older man, "I'll do what I can to help you get there."

"Sir," replied the young attorney, "I go to Springfield absolutely unpledged, or I don't go at all."

Did you hear about the girl with the Supreme Court figure?

No appeal.

* * *

The lawyer's wife confided to her maid, "I think my husband is having an affair with the stenographer."

"I don't believe it," the maid gasped. "You're only saying that to get me jealous."

* * *

To celebrate the opening of his new law office, Hartman's family gave him a dinner party. The young lawyer's ultra-bright nephew got on him immediately. "If a man had a peacock, and it went into another man's yard and laid an egg, who would the egg belong to?"

Everyone at the table looked at the new lawyer for the brightest answer ever to issue from his lips.

"That's easy," said Hartman. "The egg would belong to the man who owned the peacock. But he could be prosecuted for trespassing if he went on the other man's property to retrieve the egg."

"A helluva lawyer you'll make," snapped the youngster. "Didn't you know that a peacock can't lay an egg?"

There was a young lawyer named Rex
Who was sadly deficient in sex.
    Arraigned for exposure,
    He said with composure,
"De minimis non curat lex."
(The law is not concerned with trifles.)

\*   \*   \*

Mrs. Shaffer went to the governor of her state and said to him, "Governor, I want to get my husband out of prison."

"What is he in prison for?" asked the state leader.

"For stealing a loaf of bread," said the woman.

"Is he a good husband?" asked the governor.

"No, sir," she replied. "He drinks, he beats the children, and he's no good."

"Then why do you want him out of jail?"

"Well," she responded, "we're out of bread again."

\*   \*   \*

SOLICITOR'S SONG

*She was only a lawyer's daughter,*
*but she went from bar to bar.*

Did you hear about the lawyer who was so successful he had his own ambulance?

* * *

Quimby, the great trial lawyer, married a beautiful blonde he had saved from a long prison term. After a year, he began to suspect she was untrue to him.

Forced to leave town for a weekend business trip, Quimby explained the problem to his partner Gellman and asked him to keep an eye on the wife while he was away.

When he returned, Quimby demanded to know what happened.

"Well," said Gellman, "the night you left, a good-looking guy picked her up at the house, and they went to a nightclub. I followed them and saw them drinking together and dancing very closely. Around three in the morning, they got into a cab, and I could see them hugging and smooching in the back seat. I followed them back to your house, and through the window I could see them kissing and fondling each other. Then they went into the bedroom and switched off the lights, so I couldn't see anymore."

"That's the trouble," exclaimed the lawyer, "always that element of doubt!"

* * *

George Bernardi, the brilliant Colorado investment counselor, breaks up clients with this belly buster:

A cruise ship was wrecked in a storm. Next morning, the survivors found themselves on a desert island without food or water. They noticed the wreckage of the ship on a sandbar only 500 yards from the shore, but there were sharks swimming all around the inlet.

"I'll swim out and get food," volunteered a young man. "I used to be a lifeguard."

He dove into the water and in a few minutes was attacked and devoured by the sharks. Another man stepped forward. "I'm only a CPA, but I'm a strong swimmer. I can make it."

But he didn't. Forty yards offshore, the sharks tore him apart. Suddenly, up stepped a paunchy, bespectacled, bald-headed man. "I'm a lawyer, and I think I can get to the ship."

He entered the water, and immediately eight sharks formed a two-lane escort and helped him to the ship and back, unharmed.

"Good heavens!" shouted one of the passengers. "It's a miracle!"

"Miracle, hell!" said the lawyer. "It's just professional courtesy."

# AMERICA THE BEAUTIFUL

*Home of the brave
and land of the fee*

\* \* \*

Fuller was spending the summer in a tiny Vermont town. One morning, he approached Nelson, a weatherbeaten old-timer. "Excuse me," said Fuller, "are you a resident here?"

"Yeah," said the senior citizen, "I've lived in this town goin' on fifty years. What kin I do for you?"

"I am looking for a criminal lawyer," said the visitor. "Have you any here?"

"Well," said the old man, "we're pretty sure we have, but we can't prove it."

\* \* \*

# LAW CLERK'S CANTATA

*She was only a lawyer's daughter,
but she sure gave me a case.*

\* \* \*

*  *  *

Bob Landis, the likable Larchmont Boulevard department-store mogul, loves this lollapalooza:

Reverend Kilgore and Werner, an attorney, sat next to each other on a jet to Phoenix.

"Do you ever make mistakes in pleading?" asked the minister.

"I do," replied Werner.

"And what do you do about them?" inquired Reverend Kilgore.

"Why, if large ones, I mend them; if small ones, I let them go," said the lawyer. "Do you ever make mistakes in preaching?"

"Yes, I have."

"And what do you do?" said Werner.

"I dispose of them in the same manner as you do," answered the holy man. "Recently, as I was preaching, I meant to say that the devil was 'the father of liars,' but instead I said, 'the father of lawyers.' The mistake was so small that I let it go."

*  *  *

Pockriss went to Judge Yoss to complain that the client for whom he had just won a case refused to pay his fee.

"Did you present your request in writing?" asked Yoss.

"Yes, I did, sir," replied Pockriss.

"What did he have to say?" continued the judge.

"He told me to go to the devil," answered the lawyer.

"Then what did you do?"

"I came straight to you, sir."

\* \* \*

# agistrate Mirth

Fowler, the defendant, stood before Judge Axelrod in the county courtroom.

"You assaulted this man just because he differed from you in an argument," stated the judge. "Isn't that so?"

"I couldn't help it, Your Honor," said the defendant. "The man is a real idiot."

"You will have to pay a fine of $200 and costs," said the magistrate. "And in the future try and remember that idiots are human beings just like you and me."

\* \* \*

Susan Roth, the stunning scholarly schoolmarm, gets screams from her Los Angeles students with this sparkler:

Harriet was brought into Judge Becker's traffic court to answer a summons she'd been given for passing a red light.

"Your Honor," said the young woman, "could you dispose of my case as quickly as possible? I'm a schoolteacher, and I've got to get back to my classes."

"You're a teacher, eh?" said Becker. "I've waited years to have a schoolteacher in this court. Sit down at that table and write 'I went through a red light' five hundred times!"

Hon. Richard L. Wells, who presides at Los Angeles Federal Court, loves this wisp of whimsy:

Judge Sawyer summoned the defense attorney to the bench and said, "What does the witness mean by the expression 'Sez you'?"

"It's a slang term," explained the lawyer, "that has attained regrettable popularity in our language through the deceptive contribution of motion pictures and television and is employed to indicate a state of discredence in the witness's mind as to the fidelity or conceivability of one of my statements."

"Oh, yeah!" said the judge.

* * *

*Judge:* You are charged with pushing your mother-in-law out the window of her twenty-sixth floor apartment.

*Pierce:* I done it without thinking, sir.

*Judge:* Yes, but don't you see how dangerous it might have been for anyone passing at the time?

* * *

A man was arraigned for assault and battery and brought before Judge Maxwell:

*Maxwell:* What is your name, occupation, and what are you charged with?

*Prisoner:* My name is Sparks; I am an electrician, and I'm charged with battery.

*Maxwell:* Eh—eh—Officer, put this guy in a dry cell.

\* \* \*

Campbell, age seventy-four, was hauled into night court.

"You're charged with being intoxicated and disorderly," snapped the judge. "Have you anything to say?"

"Conscience doth makes cowards of us all," intoned Campbell. "I am not so depraved as Fitzgerald, so dissolute as Kipling, so ungrateful as Hemingway, so demented as Galsworthy, so tasteless as Shakespeare—"

"That's enough," interrupted the judge. "Ten days. And bailiff, make a list of the names he mentioned and round 'em all up. They're just as bad as he is."

\* \* \*

*Judge:* What is this man charged with?

*Officer:* Intoxication, Your Honor.

*Prisoner:* Judge, I'm as sober as you are this minute.

*Judge:* Pleads guilty—ten days! Next case.

Reynolds and Weinstein, two judges, were arrested for speeding. When they arrived in court, nobody else was present, so they decided to try each other. Reynolds went up on the stand. "How do you plead to the charge?"

"Guilty," replied Weinstein.

"Fine $50," said Reynolds, and changed places. Weinstein then asked his colleague, "How do you plead to the charge?"

"Guilty."

"Well," said Weinstein. "These cases are becoming much too common. This is the second case like this we've had this morning. I hereby fine you $100 and thirty days in jail."

\* \* \*

Just after Oklahoma was admitted to the Union, an old Indian fighter was appointed a judge. The first case before him was a man charged with horse stealing. When all the witnesses and evidence against the alleged thief were heard, the defendant's lawyer stepped up to present the defense.

"There's no point in you sayin' anything now," said the old judge. "The evidence is all in, and you'd only confuse the jury if you got talkin'."

* * *

Down South, Judge Hooper had just been appointed by his friend the new governor. Hooper had hardly any legal experience, and his first trial was a real dogfight. When the plaintiff's lawyer wound up his case, the judge said, "Defense need not speak. Plaintiff wins."

"But, Your Honor," said the defense lawyer, "at least allow me to present my case!"

"Okay," said Hooper. "Go ahead."

The defense attorney presented a well-prepared, unarguable case. When he finished, the judge shook his head in astonishment.

"Well, ain't that something," he asked. "Now, the defendant wins!"

* * *

An oil-property claim was pending in Montana before a judge who was known for his free and easy brand of justice. One day, His Honor announced:

"Gentlemen, this court has in hand a check from the plaintiff in this case for $30,000 and a check from the defendant for $20,000. The court will return $10,000 to the plaintiff. Then we will try the case strictly on its merits."

* * *

Yolanda and Fernando stood before Judge Rojeck, waiting to be married.

"This license is not filled out properly," shouted Rojeck. "Take it back downstairs to the clerk."

Yolanda and Fernando trudged down five flights of stairs to the clerk, then climbed back up to the judge's chambers. "I can't marry you," exclaimed His Honor. "The clerk forgot to sign it."

Again, the Mexican couple staggered down and then back up the steep stairs. "Okay," said the magistrate, "let's see. This marriage license still isn't filled out properly. You take it back down to the clerk and have him do it all over again!"

The exhausted couple once more made the five-flight trip. "Now," said Rojeck, looking over the license, "I think we can proceed." Suddenly, he noticed a little boy hanging on to the woman's skirt.

"Who's that child?" exclaimed the judge.

"He belong to us," said Fernando.

"I suppose you realize that in the eyes of the law he's a bastard!"

"That funny," said the Mexican, "the *señor* downstairs said you was!"

* * *

Rolf Brookes, the brainy Cincinnati bank veep, breaks up golf buddies with this beaut:

A man charged with stealing an automobile and killing a guard during a holdup near the Arkansas-Texas boundary line was captured and brought before the justice of the peace.

"We got two kinds of law in this court, son, Texas law and Arkansas law. Which'll you have?"

"I'll take Arkansas law," said the prisoner.

"Then," said the justice, "I discharge you for stealing the auto and order you put to death for killing the man."

"Hold it, judge," protested the prisoner. "I might've been a little hasty. If you don't mind, I'd like to switch to Texas law."

"It's your Constitutional right," said the justice. "So under the Texas law I discharge you for killing the man but order you put to death for stealing the auto."

* * *

Miss Hubbard, a spinster, was called to the stand. She was very attractive but no longer young.

"Let the witness state her age," said the judge, "after which she may be sworn."

* * *

Chuck Sill, the handsome Hancock Park resident, tells neighbors this humdinger:

An English solicitor was on holiday in Washington, D.C., from his London office. While at a cocktail party, he struck up a conversation with an American barrister.

"We are terribly impressed with the way your Supreme Court functions," said the Englishman. "They are truly a splendid body of men."

"That may be so," answered the lawyer. "I won't say how old some of those justices are or mention any names, but last year one of them spent the entire session trying to get out of his car!"

* * *

After a first-class donnybrook took place in a Bronx apartment house, several women appeared in court. Each accused the other of causing the trouble in the building. The judge, with Solomonlike wisdom, called for orderly testimony. "I'll hear the oldest first," he decreed.

The case was dismissed for lack of evidence.


* * *


"Have you ever been sent to prison?" asked the magistrate.

"No, Your Honor," said the prisoner, sobbing.

"Now, now, don't cry," said the judge. "You're going to be sent now."


* * *


"Are all the TV cameramen here?"

"Yes, Your Honor."

"Is the lighting set?"

"Yes, Your Honor."

"Is the sound good?"

"Yes, Your Honor."

"Good! Then let justice take its course."

*Judge:* It seems to me that I have seen you before.

*Prisoner:* You have, Your Honor; I gave your daughter singing lessons.

*Judge:* Twenty years.

\* \* \*

In Detroit, Mrs. Karnicki was on trial for beating up her husband. "What happened?" asked the judge.

"Mr. Karnicki got me to leave my job at the factory," she explained, "and come all the way home. Then he took me upstairs, got me to take off all my clothes and lie down on the bed, and then said, 'April Fool!' and walked out!"

"Case dismissed!" declared the judge.

\* \* \*

Maureen, an elderly prostitute, stood before newly elected Judge Leland. Her appeal for leniency was so convincing Leland had qualms about sentencing her. He called a short recess, then went to the chambers of an older judge. "Say, Shelby," he asked, "what would you give a sixty-year-old prostitute?"

"Oh," said the learned jurist, "no more than three dollars."

\* \* \*

Judge Bradwell decided to celebrate his seventy-eighth birthday with a surprise visit to his mistress, Yvette. He entered the apartment and found her making love to Dobson, a young lawyer.

The old jurist became hysterical and demanded satisfaction. "Wait," shouted Yvette, "I have a better way to duel. I'll dance naked in front of both of you. The first one to show a physical reaction will be the winner."

The competition began, but Dobson noticed that the judge was cheating by using his hand to help. "I object, Your Honor!" shouted the attorney. "You're tampering with the witness!"

"Objection overruled!!" bellowed Bradwell. "I was just trying to refresh the witness's memory."

\* \* \*

When the judge, with his wife having
    sport,
Proved suddenly two inches short,
    The good woman declined,
    And the judge had her fined
By proving contempt of the court.

\* \* \*

Mrs. Thorpe, an obnoxious dowager, protested her innocence to the judge. "I was not going sixty-five miles an hour," she said indignantly. "Not forty nor thirty nor ten. In fact, when the officer came up, I was almost at a standstill."

"Stop right there," warned the judge, "or you'll be backing into something."

\* \* \*

Judge Fairfield faced the jury and angrily asked, "In view of the evidence, what possible excuse can you give for acquitting this man?"

"Insanity, Your Honor," replied the foreman.

"All twelve of you?" cried the judge.

\* \* \*

He had a lusty wild career
That famous old Judge French
Because he tried a lot of girls
Down on the old park bench.

*  *  *

"Your Honor," said the prisoner when asked for an explanation, "I can't figure how I can be accused of forgery when I can't even write my own name."

"You are not charged with signing your own name," replied the judge.

*  *  *

A famous judge came late to court
  One day in busy season,
Whereat his clerk, in great surprise,
  Inquired, "What's the reason?"
"A child was born," His Honor said,
  "And I'm the happy sire."
"An infant judge?" "Oh, no," he said.
  "As yet he's but a crier."

43

Judge Whitby was hearing a paternity case involving twins.

"Twins?" asked Whitby.

"Yes, sir," replied the mother. "Both boys."

"How do you tell them apart?" asked the judge.

"This one," said the mother, pointing, "is this, and that one is that one there."

"But," said the judge, pointing, "couldn't this one be this, also?"

"Yes," said the mother. "Then, of course, that one could be that."

"How do you manage to separate them?"

"We seldom do," explained the mother, "but when we want to, we put one in one room and the other twin in another room."

"How do you know which one you're putting in each room?"

"We look and see which is in the other room and then we know the other is in the other room."

"But if one of them was in the house, and the other was away somewhere, would you be able to tell which was in the house?"

"Oh, yes," said the mother. "We'd just look at him, and then we'd know the one we saw was the one in the house. Naturally, the one away somewhere would be the other. There are only two of them, which makes it easy."

"Yes," wailed Whitby. "If they were quintuplets I'd be on a psychiatrist's couch."

McGee Grisby, the champion golfer/attorney, remembers this witty winner:

Judge Everett was considering the verdict in the paternity suit before him.

The courtroom was silent. Then suddenly he reached into the folds of his robes, drew out a cigar, and ceremoniously handed it to the defendant.

"Congratulations!" said the jurist. "You have just become a father!"

*   *   *

While on his rounds, Officer Sullivan stumbled on a young couple making love in a graveyard. The policeman promptly carted them off to night court. "What were you doing in a graveyard at midnight?" asked Magistrate Ridley.

"Nothing wrong, Your Honor," replied the boy. "We were just burying the old stiff."

"And how about you?" Ridley asked the girl.

"I was the undertaker," she responded.

"You idiot!" exclaimed the judge to the policeman. "I fine you $25 for disturbing the piece."

*   *   *

Did you hear about the two gay judges that tried each other?

* * *

Judge Moinahan wanted very much to be reelected to his post. At a democratic-club luncheon, he stood up and said, "It has been my endeavor to administer justice without swerving to partiality on the one hand or impartiality on the other hand."

* * *

A tiny Texas town was catapulted into the national limelight because of the trial of a teenage ranch hand. Reporters from every major newspaper in the country were in the courtroom along with newscasters from the network radio and television stations.

The boy had murdered his parents with an ax and then shot his girl friend Sally. After that, he broke her mother's leg and then stabbed to death Sally's father and two brothers. The judge, seeing the crowd, thought he would be expected to say a few words.

He looked over the tops of his glasses and admonished, "Now, look here, son, you know you ain't been actin' right."

"Silence in the court," shouted the judge. "Half a dozen men have been convicted already without the court being able to hear a word of the testimony."

* * *

One bright morning in a Dublin courtroom, the judge became infuriated by the noise and disturbance in the public gallery. He ordered the courtroom to be cleared.

"All the scoundrels that aren't lawyers will have to leave," cried the Irishman.

* * *

"You are lying so clumsily," said the judge to the defendant, "that I would advise you to get a lawyer."

* * *

Parrish reported for jury duty and then asked to be excused because he was prejudiced.

"I took one look at those shifty eyes, Your Honor," said Parrish, "and I knew right away he was just as guilty as sin."

"Sit down," snapped the judge. "That's the lawyer."

* * *

Milt Larsen, the marvelous Magic Castle creator, conjured up this cajoler:

An Arizona judge telephoned home one afternoon, and the Mexican housekeeper answered it. "Put my wife on the phone!" demanded the magistrate.

"*Señor*," whispered the servant, "I am sorry to tell you this, but you wife is in the bedroom makin' love to you best fren' from next door."

"Listen to me carefully," snapped the judge. "Go into the den, open my desk drawer, take out the gun, and shoot both of them."

"But, *señor*, I no can do that!"

"You better do as I say or I'll come home and shoot them and you, too."

The frightened *señorita* left the phone and returned in a few minutes. "Okay, *señor*, I do what you say. I keel them both and throw the gun in the pool."

"Pool? We don't have a pool. Wait a minute. Is this 472-6380 . . . ?"

\* \* \*

The district attorney questioned a witness, "You are a barber, aren't you?"

"No," replied the witness, "I am a tonsorial artist."

"Well, now," put in the judge, "isn't that splitting hairs?"

\* \* \*

48

Kirsch and Webber opposed each other in a trial. Before it even started, they were at each other's throats. "You're a dirty shyster," snarled Kirsch, "and before this case is through, I'll show you up for the crooked baboon that you are."

"Oh, yeah," boomed Webber. "You are a cheat and a liar."

"That's enough," interrupted the judge. "Let the case proceed now that the learned counsel have identified each other."

\* \* \*

## Witness Whimsy

Judge Hanson was very severe with the woman. "You are the wife of this man," he said. "You knew he was a burglar when you married him?"

"Yes," she replied, "but I was getting old and had no choice. It was either a burglar or a lawyer."

\* \* \*

The D.A. had the beautiful blonde on the stand. "I want you to tell the court where you were on the night of June twenty-third?"

"I'll agree to tell you," she said, "if the judge'll tell where he was the same night."

"What have the actions of the judge to do with the case?"

"Nothing," she said, giggling, "but I like a little gossip just as well as you do."

*   *   *

Attorney Potter had subpoenaed a young boy as an important witness. As soon as the youngster climbed on to the witness chair, the lawyer started to fire questions at him.

"Have you an occupation?" asked Potter.

"Nope."

"What kind of work does your father do?"

"None."

"Does he ever do anything to help support the family?"

"Odd jobs once in a while."

"Then isn't your father just a worthless loafer and a deadbeat?"

"I don't know," answered the witness, "but you can ask him. He's sittin' over there in the jury."

*   *   *

*Lawyer:* You say you saw the man stabbed in the hay field with a fork. What kind of a fork?

*Witness:* Well, did you ever see a tuning fork or an oyster fork in a hay field?

*   *   *

\* \* \*

Bascomb, an Alabama farmer, was brought in to testify in a slander suit involving two of his neighbors. "Tell me the exact conversation," said the attorney.

"I can't remember it all," answered the witness, " 'cept each one was callin' the other what they both is."

\* \* \*

"Spooky" Bob Rosenthal, the lovable legal legend, tells about the judge who asked a woman witness her age.

"Thirty," she replied.

"You've given that age in this court for the last three years."

"Yes, Your Honor. I'm not one of those who says one thing today and another thing tomorrow."

\* \* \*

Francine was hauled into court on suspicion of engaging in a shady profession. "Are you innocent?" asked the magistrate.

"Certainly not, judge," she replied. "Are you?"

\* \* \*

Mark Wilson, the world-famous magic wizard, makes whoopee with this whopper:

Thurston was being badgered by Easterly, the cross-examining attorney. "You're sure it was exactly five minutes?"

"Yes, sir," answered the witness.

"I'm going to give you a test," said the lawyer, looking at his wrist watch. "Tell me when five minutes are up."

At exactly five minutes, Thurston shouted, "Right now!"

After losing the case, the lawyer, being a good sport, walked over to the witness and asked, "How could you tell time so exactly?"

"Simple," said Thurston. "By the clock up on the wall behind you."

*   *   *

Eula Mae was loyal to her boy friend Alvin even though he got into trouble. When Alvin's trial came up, she offered to act as a character witness. Eula Mae stayed very calm despite the prosecuting attorney's sizzling cross-examination.

"You claim you know the defendant well enough to be certain that he would never steal?"

"Dat's right, suh."

"Are you positive that he would never steal even if he were in desperate need of funds?"

"Ah believes that, suh!"

"Do you know what it means to be in dire need of money? Have you ever been financially embarrassed?"

"Well," answered Eula Mae, "you might say dat ah has often been pushed fo' money."

*   *   *

"You say it was nighttime," bellowed the district attorney. "You were at least three blocks away, and still you saw the defendant shoot Dillingham. How far can you see at night?"

"I don't know," said the witness. "How far is the moon?"

*   *   *

Dilfer was a little man, no more than five feet tall, yet he was accused by an Amazon of a female over six feet tall. Dilfer was charged with rape. Judge Daniels looked at the incongruity of their sizes and then spoke to the woman. "It isn't that I doubt you, madam, but you're so tall, and he's so short. It seems almost impossible that your charge could be true."

"Your Honor, it is true!" shouted the woman. "Although I admit I did stoop a little!"

\* \* \*

## OVERHEARD IN TAMPA TRAFFIC COURT

*Judge:* I'm going to let you off with a fine this time, but another day I'll send you to jail.

*Driver:* Sort of a weather forecast, eh, Your Honor?

*Judge:* What do you mean?

*Driver:* Fine today—cooler tomorrow.

\* \* \*

*Lawyer* (to rattled witness): Did you, or did you not, on the aforementioned day, Friday, November fourth, feloniously and with malicious aforethought listen at the keyhole of the tenth-floor front condominium, then occupied as a residence by the defendant in this action on Eighty-sixth Street near West End Avenue, and did you not also, on the Wednesday following the Friday in November before referred to, communicate to your wife the information acquired and repeat the conversation overheard on that occasion with the result that the gossip of your wife gave wide and far currency to the overheard conversation before mentioned? Did you, or did you not? Answer yes or no.

*Witness:* Huh?

\* \* \*

Butler, the defense lawyer in a robbery case, was cross-examining a witness.

"When did the robbery take place?" demanded the counsel.

"I think—" began the witness.

"We don't care what you think, sir," interrupted Butler. "We want to know what you know."

"Then if you don't want to know what I think," said the witness, "I might as well leave the stand: I can't talk without thinking—I'm not a lawyer."

\* \* \*

Alan Saltzman, the illustrious Los Angeles attorney, tells about a colleague who was quizzing the defendant.

"After you poisoned the coffee, your husband sat at the breakfast table with you and sipped it. Didn't you feel the slightest bit of pity for him?"

"Yes," she answered. "There was just one moment when I felt sorry for him."

"When was that?" asked the lawyer.

"When he asked for his second cup."

* * *

"Haven't I seen you before?" asked the judge.

"Maybe," replied the tailor. "So many men owe me money, I can't remember their faces."

* * *

Young Jamie, a witness in an accident case, was queried by a lawyer. "Did anyone tell you what to say in court?"

"Yes, sir."

"I thought so. Who was it?"

"My father, sir."

"And what did he tell you?"

"He said the lawyers would try to get me all tangled up, but if I stuck to the truth, I would be all right."

* * *

McKinley asked the witness, "Are you acquainted with any members of the jury?"

"Yeah," he grumbled, "more than half."

"Are you willing to swear that you know more than half of them?"

"If it comes to that," replied the witness, "I'll swear that I know more than all of them put together."

* * *

Kramer had been subpoenaed as a witness in a trial for an assault. The lawyer, who was notorious for browbeating witnesses, asked him what distance he was from the parties when the assault happened.

"Just thirteen feet eleven inches and a half."

"How can you be so exact?" said the counsel.

"I expected some idiot lawyer would ask me," said the witness, "so I measured it."

* * *

\* \* \*

Judge Fournier removed his glasses, leaned toward the witness, and said, "Do you understand that you are swearing to tell the truth?"

"Yes, sir."

"And do you know what will happen if you do not tell the truth?"

"Yes, sir," replied the witness. "Our side will win the case."

\* \* \*

In Oklahoma City, Leighton was charged with shooting some pigeons that belonged to Holzer, a farmer. Leighton's lawyer tried to frighten the farmer.

"Now," said the counselor, "are you prepared to swear that this man shot your pigeons?"

"I didn't say he shot 'em," replied Holzer. "I said I suspected him of doing it."

"Ah! Now we're coming to it. What made you suspect Mr. Leighton?"

"First off, I caught him on my land with a gun. Second, I heard a gun go off and saw some pigeons fall. And third, I found four of my pigeons in his pocket, and I don't think the birds flew there and committed suicide."

"You've heard what the last witness said," challenged the counsel, "and yet your evidence is completely contrary. Am I to assume that you wish to throw doubt on her veracity?"

"Not at all," he replied. "I simply wish to make it clear what a liar I am if she's speaking the truth."

* * *

Babitz was telling Halstead, a colleague, about his courtroom experience that day. "I had Dr. Migdall, the brilliant authority on internal medicine, against me in the case," said the lawyer. "All that the court would allow me was a hypothetical question."

"Go on," prompted Halstead.

"Our office worked on the question for weeks. We checked all possible answers against the most authoritative medical opinion. Finally, in court today, I took one full hour to ask the question."

"So?" asked the other attorney.

"And then I finished—"

"Yes?"

"The witness asked me—"

"Yes?"

"If I would mind repeating the question."

* * *

A rough-looking Kansas City hoodlum was being sworn in as a witness in court.

"Do you promise to tell the truth, the whole truth, and nothing but the truth, so help you God!" said the clerk.

"Why not?" said the tough guy. "I'll try anything once."

* * *

Hoffmann developed a reputation for bullying witnesses. One day at a trial in Boston, he met his match. Mrs. Quinlan, a huge Irish woman, testified that she awoke in the morning and found the accused lying beside her and discovered that she had been raped.

"Now, madame," goaded Hoffmann, "if one may take so preposterous an accusation as that seriously, you might even charge it upon me. Let us suppose you should wake up and find me lying beside you. What would you think?"

"I'd think I'd had a miscarriage!" exclaimed Mrs. Quinlan.

* * *

George Voorhis, McDonald's number-one "Ronald," clowns around with this cackler:

Ingram was sure he had caught the witness in a lie and wanted to capitalize on the point. Ingram strode arrogantly toward the witness stand and in a cold, domineering voice snarled, "You say that the fence was eight feet high? And you were standing on the ground?" he asked.

"Yes, sir," said the witness.

"You weren't mounted on a ladder or anything?"

"No, sir," replied the witness.

The counselor pointed his finger at the man and shouted, "Would you explain, then, how you, a man of little over five feet, could see over a fence eight feet high and watch the accused's actions."

"Yes," said the witness. "There was a hole in the fence."

The Cincinnati murder trial was nearing its climax. On the witness stand was Rita, a gorgeous redhead. The prosecuting attorney glared at her.

"I'll repeat my question," he thundered. "Where were you on the night of January twenty-second?"

"Oh, please don't ask me that," retorted Rita. "I can't tell you."

"You must tell us," he roared. "Where were you on the night of January twenty-second?"

"All right," said the beauty, "if you must know, I'll tell you. I was at home, working out a crossword puzzle."

"Is that anything to be ashamed of?"

"Of course, it is," she answered, sobbing. "A beautiful girl like me, wasting a night on a crossword puzzle."

* * *

Another woman was asked by a Denver judge, "Have you ever appeared as a witness in this suit before?"

"Oh, no, Your Honor," she exclaimed. "The last time I testified, I wore my pink Christian Dior blouse with my black Gucci skirt."

* * *

Woodhill, age seventy-eight, was called as a witness. "Mr. Woodhill," said the lawyer, "did you or did you not, on the date in question or at any time previously or subsequently, say or even intimate to the defendant or anyone else, whether friend or mere acquaintance or, in fact, a stranger, that the statement imputed to you, whether just or unjust and denied by the plaintiff, was a matter of the moment or otherwise? Answer: Did you, or did you not?"

"Did I, or did I not what?" asked the old man.

\* \* \*

McNichol tried to challenge a witness by asking, "The truth of the matter is that you are not an unbiased, objective witness, isn't it? You, too, were shot in the fracas?"

"No, sir," replied the witness, "I was shot midway between the fracas and the navel."

\* \* \*

"How long have you known the defendant?"

"Twelve years."

"Tell the court whether you think he is the type of man who would steal this money or not."

"How much was it?"

* * *

In a South Carolina courtroom, Milbank was questioning the witness, Farmer Stump.

"I understand you called on the plaintiff."

"Yes," answered the farmer.

"What did you say?"

Prosecutor Pollard leaped to his feet and bellowed, "That question is false, misleading, and tends to incriminate an entirely innocent party. The attorney for the defense is using illegal tactics. Besides being an immoral person, he is guilty of malicious practices in trying to introduce such testimony. He's also a no-good bastard!"

Milbank jumped on the prosecutor, and the two men slugged it out all over the courtroom. The judge rapped for order, and finally court attendants separated the two members of the bar. Each man had a bloody nose and two black eyes. Then the judge ruled that if Milbank would repeat the question, the witness was required to answer it.

"I repeat, then," said the lawyer, wiping blood from his upper lip. "What did you say?"

"I didn't say nuttin'," answered the farmer. "He weren't home."

*   *   *

The judge wished to make sure that the witness understood the solemnity of the occasion.

"Do you know what that oath means?" the judge asked.

"Sure I do," replied the witness. "That oath means if I swear to a lie, I gotta stick to it."

*   *   *

Dawkins, a Georgia bus driver, was arrested for shooting a man. The next morning, he was brought into court.

"Why did you shoot that man?" asked the judge.

" 'Cause he called me a black sonuvabitch!"

"You can't go and shoot a man for that!"

"Well, judge, what would you have done if he called you that?"

"Oh, he wouldn't have called me that!"

"I know, judge, but suppose he'd called you the kind of a sonuvabitch you is?"

*   *   *

McCormick, the defense attorney, was cross-examining Rogers.

"You say you met the defendant on a streetcar and that he had been drinking and gambling?"

"Yes," replied the witness.

"Did you see him take a drink?"

"No."

"Did you see him gambling?"

"No."

"Then how do you know," prompted the attorney, "that the defendant had been drinking and gambling?"

"Well," explained Rogers, "he gave the bus driver a blue chip for his bus fare and told him to keep the change."

\* \* \*

Farmer Winslow, a witness in a hog-stealing case, seemed to be stretching things in favor of the accused.

"Do you know the nature of an oath?" demanded the prosecuting attorney.

"Yeah."

"Are you aware that you must not bear false witness against your neighbor?"

"I'm not bearin' false witness against him. I'm bearin' false witness for him."

\* \* \*

The witness was being cross-examined, and Kelem asked the same question again and again. Everyone grew impatient, particularly the witness.

"You say that after the auto passed, you saw the victim lying there in the street with his scalp bleeding?"

"Yes, I did."

"After the auto passed?"

"Yes."

"But did the car hit him?"

"Yes."

"Are you sure?"

"No. What I said was a lie. The driver leaned out and bit him as the car went by."

\* \* \*

"Otis, do you solemnly swear to tell the truth, the whole truth, and nothing but the truth?"

"Ah does, sah."

"Well, Otis, what have you got to say for yourself?"

"Jedge, wif all dem limitations you jes' put on me, Ah don't believe Ah has anything at all to say."

\* \* \*

McCoy became insidiously sarcastic in his cross-examination, but the woman who was in the witness box remained calm.

"You say you had no education, but you answered my questions smartly enough."

"You don't have to be no scholar to answer silly questions," replied the witness.

\* \* \*

Mrs. Edwards was a witness in a murder trial. "I'd like to tell the story in my own way," she complained to the judge. "Without the interruptions of that slick-looking shyster—"

"Just a minute," said the judge. "Madam, you must not refer to the counsel for the defendant in such terms."

"I'm sorry," she apologized. "I just wanna tell what I saw without being stopped by that—say, what was that fancy name you gave that slick-looking shyster?"

\* \* \*

Benson was being interrogated rudely by Smolens, the plaintiff's attorney.

"What did you say your business was?" asked Smolens.

"I'm a short-order cook in a diner," replied Benson.

"A short-order cook?" snarled the lawyer. "What would you consider your social status is in this world as a short-order cook?"

"Not very high," said the witness, "but I feel I'm doing better than my father before me."

"What was your father?"

"He was a shyster lawyer," said Benson.

\* \* \*

## *Shyster Shenanigans*

Lampert the attorney leaped to his feet and shouted, "I object to everything he said!"

"Why?" asked the judge.

"It makes it sound as if I was listening."

\* \* \*

Norvel and Speckles, two lawyers, met at a cocktail party. "How's business?" asked Norvel.

"Rotten!" answered Speckles. "Yesterday I chased an ambulance twenty miles. When I caught up, there was another lawyer already in it."

\* \* \*

Dinelli rushed into court and asked that a new trial be granted his client, who had been found guilty the day before. "I've uncovered new evidence," he told the judge.

"What kind?" asked the judge.

"My client has an extra $2,000, and I found out about it only this morning," replied Dinelli.

* * *

## LAWYER

*A fellow who is willing to go
out and spend your last cent
to prove he is right*

* * *

"Here's my bill," said Gassner. "Please give me $5,000 as a down payment and then $500 a month thereafter for twelve months."

"Sounds like buying an automobile," said the client.

"I am," returned the attorney.

* * *

Barton took his dog to the Wilkins Obedience School. "You can have your dog trained to be anything," said Wilkins.

"What do you mean?" asked Barton.

Wilkins took a bunch of bones, dropped them on the ground, and whistled for a dog. The animal jogged out, grabbed the bones, and in a few moments had built a house. "Now that dog belongs to an architect," announced the dog trainer.

"Amazing!" said Barton.

Wilkins dismantled the bones, threw them on the ground, and released another dog. This time, the canine built a skeleton. "He's owned by a doctor!" said Wilkins.

"That's incredible," blurted out Barton.

Suddenly, a third dog wandered out. This one ate the bones and then screwed both dogs.

"Good heavens!" shouted Barton. "Who owns that one?"

"Oh, that dog belongs to a divorce lawyer!"

\* \* \*

A psychological test was prepared to see how members of different professions would answer the same question. An engineer and a lawyer were called in. The examiner asked the engineer, "How much is two times two?"

The engineer replied, "Three point nine, nine, nine, nine . . ."

Then he asked the lawyer, "How much is two times two?"

The lawyer said, "How much do you want it to be?"

Soriano the cripple thumped his crutch on the office floor as he confronted Conrad. "Your bill is outrageous!" he exclaimed. "You're taking four-fifths of my damages. I never heard of such extortion."

"I furnished the skill, the eloquence, and the necessary legal learning for your case," said Conrad.

"Yes," said the client, "but I furnished the case itself."

"That's ridiculous!" sneered the lawyer. "Anybody could fall down a manhole."

\* \* \*

## PERSISTENT LAWYER

*One who wouldn't hesitate to spend
an entire evening trying to break
a girl's will*

\* \* \*

Ellison had a lawsuit involving a property title. When he walked into the courtroom, Silverman, his opponent, came over to him. "Are those your witnesses sitting over there?"

"They are," said Ellison.

"Then you win," said the other lawyer, "I've used those witnesses twice myself."

\* \* \*

*First Lawyer:* As soon as I realized it was crooked business, I got out of it.

*Second Lawyer:* How much?

\* \* \*

What's the difference between a rooster and a shyster?

A rooster clucks defiance.

Barrison, a young lawyer who had taken over his father's practice, rushed home one evening rather elated. "Dad, listen," he shouted. "I've settled that old Hazlett suit at last."

"*Settled it*!" cried the astonished parent. "Why I gave you that as *an annuity* for your life."

* * *

Underwood was relaxing at his club. "Say, do you think it'll rain?" he asked Brewster, a lawyer sitting next to him.

"I wouldn't say so," answered Brewster. The next day, Underwood received a bill for legal advice.

A week later, they met again at the club, and Underwood casually said, "Think we're going to have war with Russia?"

"I doubt it," replied the lawyer.

The next day, his bill arrived at Underwood's home.

Underwood took the second bill and rushed to the club. He found Brewster relaxing in an armchair and stormed up to him.

"Listen, you shyster, you're a crook!" he shouted. "And remember, I'm not *asking*, I'm *telling*!"

* * *

* * *

"I am beginning to think my lawyer is too interested in seeing how much money he can get out of me."

"Why do you say that?"

"Listen to this: 'Bill: For waking up at night and thinking about your case: $25.' "

* * *

"Before I take your case," said the counselor, "you'll have to give me a $50 retainer."

"All right, here's the $50," agreed Nyman, handing over the money.

"Thank you," the lawyer retorted. "This entitles you to two questions!"

"What! Fifty dollars for just two questions! Isn't that awfully high?"

"Yes, I suppose it is," said the lawyer. "Now what's your second question?"

* * *

Two County Cork barristers were sipping some brew at a popular pub.

"Timothy's developin' quite a reputation!"

"That he is. Ever since three of his clients were hung, he's known as 'Swing and Sway with Briefcase O'Shay.' "

\* \* \*

## LAWYER

*A man who helps you get
what's coming to him*

\* \* \*

Hernandez, who shot a fellow in a barroom dispute, wired to Philadelphia for a lawyer to defend him. The answer came:
ARRIVING BY PLANE TOMORROW.
BRINGING TWO EYEWITNESSES.

\* \* \*

"Tell me about your first case."
"I borrowed $20,000 from my father so I could study law."
"So?"
"After I started practice, my father sued me for $20,000."

\* \* \*

Did you hear about the lawyer who was hurt in an accident?
The ambulance backed up suddenly.

\* \* \*

Mildred entered a drugstore and said to the attendant, "I bought a bottle of internal cleanser that you recommended, and that stuff burned my insides."

"We just sell it, lady," said the attendant. "We don't make it."

"I'm going to a lawyer," she said.

She explained the circumstances, and the attorney said, "All right, we'll sue for $10,000 and expenses. What business are you in?"

"I'm a prostitute," she replied.

"Sorry," he said, "but I can't handle your case."

She tried several lawyers, but none would take her case. Finally, she ended up with a shyster known for his disreputable clientele. "We'll sue for $100,000 and attorney's fees," he said. "What business are you in?"

"Well," she replied, "I'm a hooker."

"Even better," he admitted. "We'll make that $200,000 and institute a second suit for arson."

"Arson?" she asked.

"Sure!" he smiled. "We'll claim they burned up your business."

* * *

84

A famous Honolulu lawyer was called in to see a man in the county jail accused of murder.

When he returned to his office, his young law clerk said, "Well, did you take the case, Mr. Parker?"

"No, I didn't."

"Why? Didn't you think the man was justified in his act?"

"My son," said the lawyer, "he certainly was not financially justified in committing murder."

\* \* \*

85

# *Court Jesters*

Simpson asked to be excused from jury duty. "I owe a man $100 that I borrowed," he explained, "and since he's leavin' town today for some years, I wanna catch him before he gets to the plane and pay him the money."

"You are excused," announced the judge. "I don't want anybody on the jury who can lie like you."

* * *

## JURY

*A group of twelve men selected
to decide who has the better
lawyer*

* * *

The trial ended, and the jury retired to render its decision. They were out for such a long time, Judge Moore sent the bailiff to check up.

"How are things going?" asked Moore.

"They report that they are standing ten to two, Your Honor."

"For which verdict?" asked the judge.

"I can't be sure, but as I was leaving, they were taking up a collection for the prisoner's widow."

* * *

Judge Cordell became thoroughly disgusted with a jury that seemed unable to reach a verdict in what appeared to be an open and shut case. Finally, he said, "I discharge this jury."

Hammond, a very sensitive member, indignantly faced the magistrate and roared, "You can't discharge me!"

"And why not?" snapped the judge.

"Because," said the juror, pointing to the lawyer for the defense, "I was hired by that man."

*   *   *

*Zachary:* Your Honor, I don't think I can serve on the jury. One look at that man there convinces me he's guilty.

*Judge:* Quiet! That is the district attorney.

*   *   *

David Huddleston, the talented TV actor, tells about the judge who was furious with a jury that could not reach a decision. He really lowered the boom on them. "You did not pay close attention. You failed to grasp legal fundamentals. You ought to be ashamed of yourselves."

"Please, judge, don't be peeved at me," said an old man in the rear of the jury box. "I'm the only one on your side."

*   *   *

Cordell showed up for jury duty and had been examined by both defense and prosecution. He was about to be accepted when the prosecutor asked, "Do you believe in capital punishment?"

"Well, sir, I do," said Cordell, "if it ain't too severe."

*   *   *

Herb Schwartz, the brilliant tax-planning attorney, beams over this bubbler:

This had nothing to do with Women's Lib. It just turned out that way. An all-female jury was picked in Portland, Oregon, for a murder trial. The lawyers had rested their cases, and the verdict had been in the hands of the twelve women for twenty-four hours.

The judge said sternly, "After all this time, you are unable to arrive at a verdict?"

"Your Honor," said the forewoman, "we have arrived at twelve verdicts."

* * *

During a murder trial, Judge Higbie asked one prospective juror, "Have you formed any opinion concerning the guilt or innocence of the prisoner?"

"No, Your Honor, I have not."

"Have you any conscientious objections against imposing the death penalty if the prisoner is found guilty?"

"Not in this case, Your Honor," replied the juror.

* * *

Judge Kaplan, after a three-hour charge to the jury, finally said: "Are there any other questions before the jury retires?"

"Your Honor," said a woman, "please tell us what is a plaintiff and what is a defendant?"

* * *

Teague learned Fogarty would be a juror on his murder trial. He quietly paid off the Irishman to hold out for a manslaughter charge.

The jury was out a long time and finally came in with a verdict of manslaughter. Teague was overjoyed. He rushed to Fogarty's side and pumped his hand. "Was it much of a fight in there?" asked Teague.

"Terrible!" answered Fogarty. "The other eleven wanted to acquit you, but I held out for manslaughter."

There was a young man of Missouri
Who screwed with a terrible fury,
    Till hauled into court
    For his bestial sport,
And condemned by a poorly hung jury.

\* \* \*

A hush fell over the Dublin courtroom. "Have you reached a verdict?" asked the judge.

"Yes, Your Lordship," announced the foreman of the jury. "We find that the man who stole the money is not guilty."

\* \* \*

In Tel Aviv, the courtroom clatter came to an abrupt halt. The jury foreman stood up when the judge asked him if they had reached a decision. "We're all of one mind," he said. "We decided not to interfere."

\* \* \*

After a visit to the United States, a Chinese dignitary returned to Shanghai and gave his countrymen this description of American court trials: "One man is silent, another talks all the time, and twelve wise men condemn the man who has not said a word."

\* \* \*

A tiny town in the hills of Tennessee was trying its first case. The all-backwoodsmen jury had been arguing for hours. When at last they straggled back, the foreman, a tall moonshine maker, expressed the general opinion.

"We don't think he done it," he drawled, "for we allow he wasn't there; but we think he would've if he'd a had the chance."

\* \* \*

The jury had been arguing the merits of a murder trial for twenty-two straight hours. Wearily, the jury members returned to the jury box.

Before the verdict was disclosed, the foreman motioned to the judge and said, "Your Honor, may we ask a question?"

"Of course, speak up," replied the judge.

"Well," said the foreman. "Before we pass judgment, we'd like to know if the defendant prefers AC or DC current?"

\* \* \*

Billings, the most-popular farmer in a Mississippi rural community, killed a worthless drifter during a quarrel. Being an honest man, Billings pleaded guilty to first-degree murder. The punishment would obviously be hanging. But the jury, all friends of his, determined to save him in spite of himself. They brought in a verdict of not guilty.

"How in the world," said the judge, "can you bring in such a verdict when the defendant has pleaded guilty?"

"Well, Your Honor," said the foreman, "the defendant is such a liar that we can't believe him."

*  *  *

There once was a famous case in a small Montana mining town. Zirowich was being tried on an assault charge against Birdsall. The state prosecutor brought into court the weapons used: a baseball bat, a rake, brass knuckles, a bayonet, and a luger.

Birdsall's lawyer brought in the plaintiff's means of defense. A pickax, a bowie knife, a tomahawk, a shovel, and ten feet of chain.

After deliberating for fifteen minutes, the twelve men filed in slowly, and the foreman read the verdict. "We the jury would give $500 to have seen the fight."

*  *  *

* * *

"Where did the car hit him?" the doctor was asked by the attorney.

"He was struck at the junction of the dorsal and cervical vertebrae," replied the physician.

Rodriguez rose up in the jury box and called out, "I been livin' in this town forty years, and I ain't never heard of any such place around here."

* * *

The defense had closed, the prosecuting attorney had finished argument, and now Judge Reyburn, both long-winded and pompous, was charging the jury. Suddenly, he noticed Bostwick snoring in the jury box. He rapped on his desk and awakened the sleeper. Reyburn glared at him and then said sarcastically, "That's a fine way to attend to your duty. Do you think your opinion will be of any value when I send you out to determine the fate of the prisoner?"

"Yes, I think so, Your Honor," said the juryman.

"You do, huh?" shouted the judge. "Tell me, how long have you been sleeping?"

"I don't know, Your Honor," said Bostwick. "How long have you been talking?"

* * *

*Judge:* This man claims that you seduced his wife. Are you guilty?

*Accused:* I don't know. I haven't heard the evidence yet.

\* \* \*

Judge Webster was interviewing a prospective panel member. "Ever serve on a jury?"

"No, I've been too smart to get caught on a jury."

"What's that?" screamed the judge. "You boast of your smartness in escaping jury duty? That is the highest calling of a good citizen."

"Your Honor," explained the man, "I meant I was always excused because the lawyers thought I wasn't ignorant enough."

\* \* \*

In a suit against a railroad company, a West Virginia jury brought in this verdict:

"If the train had run as it should have ran; if the bell had rung as it should have rang; if the whistle had blowed as it should have blew, both of which it did neither—the cow would have not been injured when she was killed."

\* \* \*

Ed Hallberg, RCA's dynamic West Coast distribution exec, delivers this delightful dash of drollery:

Stacey, age seventy-three, had been on many juries and sat in on many trials. An attorney asked him, "Who influences you the most, the lawyers, the judge, or the witnesses?"

"Well," said the senior citizen, "I'm a plain and reasoning man, and I ain't influenced by anything the lawyers say nor by what the witnesses say or even what the judge says. I just look at the defendant, and I ask myself, 'If he ain't done nothing wrong, why's he here?' So I bring 'em all in guilty."

\* \* \*

## *Flatfoot Funnies*

Officer Moore was being interrogated by an obnoxious attorney.

"Then you dare to say that this man was drunk!" yelled the lawyer.

"No, sir," said the policeman, "I simply said he sat in his car for three hours in front of an excavation waiting for the light to turn green."

\* \* \*

POLICEMAN'S UNION

*Amalgamated Copper*

\* \* \*

Mrs. Van Nostrand tried to talk a motorcycle cop out of a ticket for speeding but to no avail.

"What do you do," she sneered, "when you find someone is *really* guilty?"

"I couldn't say, lady," he answered. "All I ever catch are the ones that are innocent!"

\* \* \*

Young Patrick looked up to a New York mounted policeman astride his horse.

"Why don't you ride in a police car?" asked the youngster.

"I would," explained the cop, "but there's no room for my horse."

\* \* \*

Officer Riley was suspected of being drunk and rowdy. One night, they brought him into the station with his uniform completely disheveled, his coat ripped down the middle, and his badge missing.

"Where's your badge?" cried the captain.

Riley glanced at his chest, then said, "The wife's using it to pin diapers on the baby."

After paying his traffic fine at the Denver Court House, the police clerk handed Norfleet a receipt.

"What am I supposed to do with this?" grumbled the motorist.

"Keep it," said the clerk. "When you get four of them, you get a bicycle."

* * *

No matter what Ralph Nader says, the best safety device is a rear-view mirror with a cop in it.

* * *

A policeman stopped Griffin driving the wrong way on a one-way street. "Didn't you see the arrow?" he demanded.

"Arrow? Honest, officer, I didn't even see the Indians."

* * *

Hurley lay on the ground.

The traffic cop asked him, "Did you get the number of the hit-and-run driver?"

"No," said Hurley, "but I'd recognize my wife's laugh anywhere."

* * *

Mal Alberts, dynamite promotion director for Steve Garvey's charity golf tournament, donated this delicious dandy:

One wintry afternoon, Officer Reardon was crossing the Verrazano Bridge on his way home to Staten Island. He spotted a man perched up on a girder ready to jump.

"C'mon down!" shouted the policeman.

No answer.

"Please, mister. If you jump, I'll have to go in after you," pleaded Reardon. "It's freezing cold, and while we're waiting for the ambulance to come, we'll both catch pneumonia, and we'll both die. Why don't you be a nice fella and go home and hang yourself!"

\* \* \*

Hudgins had been hauled into court, and now he stood shamefully before his attorney to explain his problem. "I was arrested for resisting an officer."

"Resisting an officer!" groaned the lawyer.

"Yes," said Hudgins. "I offered him twenty, and he wanted fifty."

\* \* \*

Miss Martinelli, a Bronx schoolteacher, asked her class to write an essay about New York's Finest. Herbie, one of the pupils, turned in his paper with only three words on it: *Police is bastards*.

Miss Martinelli was shocked at the boy's attitude and she arranged for the class to visit the local precinct station and see the police at work. The cops showed the children all over the station, drove them around in squad cars, let them talk to each other over the radios, and wound up the day giving them soft drinks.

Next day, the teacher asked the class to write another essay about the police force.

This time Herbie wrote: *Police is cunning bastards*.

\* \* \*

"You're trying to bribe an officer of the law! Know what I'm going to give you for it?"

"A receipt?"

* * *

While driving through a small town in a southern state, New Yorker Kirby was sideswiped by a long black Cadillac that jumped a traffic light and sped away. Kirby put down its license number and went to police headquarters to register a complaint.

The sergeant on duty looked at the number and roared, "I suppose you're gonna tell me that this guy hit you."

"That's why I'm here," said the New Yorker.

"I suppose you know the mayor personally," challenged the cop.

"I didn't say that—" began Kirby.

"And I guess you know the cousin of the chief of police?"

"Of course not!"

"And you know the brother of the political boss around here?"

"No, I don't."

"Well, put them all together," snarled the sergeant, "and they add up to the guy who hit you. Now pay me $100 for illegal parking and blocking traffic! And get out of town!"

* * *

Originally scheduled for all-night duty at the station, Patrolman Fenwick was relieved early and arrived home four hours ahead of schedule. It was nearly two A.M., and hoping to get into bed without waking his wife, he decided to undress in the dark. But as he crossed the room to climb into bed, his wife sat up and said, "Honey, would you go down to the all-night drugstore and get me some aspirin? My head is splitting."

"Sure, sweetie," he said. Feeling his way across the room, Fenwick crawled back into his clothes and stumbled out of the house and down the street to the drugstore.

As he arrived, the pharmacist looked up and said, "Excuse me, but aren't you Officer Fenwick of the Sixth Precinct?"

"Yes," said the cop.

"Then what are you doing in the fire chief's uniform?"

\* \* \*

Down South, police have always prided themselves in being courteous. In Charleston, a woman walked up to an officer and said, "Can you tell me which way to King Street?"

"I'm afraid not," said the cop. "It would mean I should have to point."

\* \* \*

"Hello, police department? I've lost my cat and—"

"Sorry, sir, that's not a job for the police. We're too busy."

"But you don't understand—this is a very intelligent cat. He's almost human. He can practically talk."

"Well, you'd better hang up, sir. He may be trying to phone you right now."

\* \* \*

"Did you notice anything special about the man?" the detective asked the bank teller after the bank was robbed for the third time by the same bandit.

"Yes, he seemed better dressed each time."

\* \* \*

A state highway patrolman near Buffalo stopped O'Neal and asked to see his driver's license. The motorist fumbled in his wallet and handed over a card.

"I want your driver's license," the officer said. "This is your library card."

"I'm looking for it," said O'Neal. "I just thought you'd like something to read 'til I find it."

\* \* \*

Officer McLean was being questioned about the drunk he arrested. The patrolman testified that the defendant said he was drunk.

*Judge:* I want his exact words. Just as the prisoner uttered them. He didn't use the pronoun he, did he?

*McLean:* Oh, yes. He said *he* was drunk.

*Judge* (impatiently): No, you don't understand. I want the very words he spoke. Did he say, ''I was drunk''?

*McLean:* You may have been drunk, judge, but the prisoner didn't mention your name.

*Prosecutor:* Look, officer, you still don't understand. The judge means, did the prisoner say to you, ''I was drunk''?

*McLean:* He might have said you were drunk, but I didn't hear him mention your name, either.

*Defense Counsel:* Here, let me try. Listen, officer, in our English syntax, our English grammar, we have three persons. The first person is I; the second person is you; and the third person is he, she, or it. Now—did my client, in his exact words, use the first person? Did he say, ''I was drunk''?

*McLean:* No, counselor, he didn't say you was drunk. He said he was drunk, and if you don't stop asking me all these questions, I'm going out and get drunk, too.

\* \* \*

The sergeant took Kowalski, the rookie patrolman, to his beat and directed, "You see that red light away up the street? You cruise between here and that light."

Kowalski did not show up at precinct headquarters for a week. When he finally did, Kowalski was disheveled and in a state of exhaustion.

"Where in the world have you been?" asked his superior.

"Sergeant," said the rookie, "you know that red light you showed me? Well, that was on a truck headed for Baltimore!"

\* \* \*

## PUBLIC SERVANT PROVERB

*Policemen have bigger balls than firemen because they sell more tickets.*

Latest statistics show that crime is on the rise in all major cities. To help combat this deplorable situation, police have begun to organize into what they call the buddy system.

Two officers were walking their beat in the Bronx when one said, ''Charlie, let's go up that dark alley and see what's makin' all that noise!''

''Not *me*, buddy!'' said his partner.

* * *

Officer Raymund was patrolling a campus lovers' lane late one night and stopped at a parked car. "What're you doin' in there?" he asked.

"We're necking," replied a man's voice.

"Well, put your neck back in your pants and get the hell outa here!"

* * *

The police station had been quiet all day and most of the week. The men were playing poker to pass the time.

"What a life," complained Sergeant Costello. "No riots, no fights, no burglaries, nothin'—not even a stabbing. If it stays quiet like this, they'll be reducing the force."

"Don't worry," said the captain. "Things will break soon. You've got to have faith in human nature."

* * *

"Hey, you hear the latest news?"

"No, what?"

"They're gonna make every police officer wear rubber boots."

"What for?"

"To keep them from waking each other up."

* * *

Said the cop at the nudist colony: "My badge is killing me!"

\* \* \*

In order to speed up the machinery to fight crime, police departments are switching over to computers and automation. One night, a man called Sixth Precinct and said, "Police! Come quick! There's a burglar downstairs, and he's putting all our valuables in a sack."

The voice on the other end said, "Keep calm! Just hang up the phone and stay where you are and a squad car will be right over! Right over! Right over! Right over!"

\* \* \*

Did you hear about the small town that elected a new police chief every year?

The first thing they did was have him arrest the old one.

\* \* \*

"How could you let him get away?" the sergeant screamed at the rookie cop. "Did you watch all the exits like I told you?"

"Yes, sir, but he must have left by one of the entrances."

\* \* \*

* * *

"Crime is booming in my neighborhood," says Will Marks, the Newark auto-repair mogul.

"My business is in a neighborhood so rough that when I called the police, there was a three-year waiting list."

* * *

A Hartford man found that some robbers can be very polite. Walking home from work one night, he was approached by a bum, who pleaded, "Please, sir. If you don't mind, sir, could you kindly spare the price of a meal? I have no work, no decent clothes—I have nothing in the world except this knife and this gun!"

* * *

New York's Mayor Koch, the wittiest and that city's best-loved leader since Fiorello La Guardia, broke up a civic dinner with:

"The increased police patrol of New York City streets has been very effective. Since it started, not a single street has been stolen."

* * *

* * *

The rookie Cambern was asked by his sergeant, "How would you go about dispersing a crowd?"

"Take up a collection," he answered. "That does it every time."

* * *

Arlene and Frank were making frenzied love in the back of his van when Officer Donovan shined his flashlight on them.

"You prying pig!" exclaimed Arlene.

"Now just a minute," declared Donovan.

"Screw yourself!" shouted the girl.

"If you don't keep a—" said the cop.

"Up yours!" screamed Arlene.

"That does it!" roared the patrolman. "Break it up there, son. You're coming along with me."

"But, officer," protested Frank, "I didn't say a word."

"That's right!" replied the cop. "But I'm taking you in, anyway—for having an offensive person on your weapon!"

* * *

Macho Morales, the Fifth Precinct's lover boy, bragged that he could seduce the pretty new policewoman, who had all the other bulls in heat. To prove his boast, Morales arranged the assignation in his police car with the short-wave radio on "transmit" so the men at the station house could hear the details.

As the two cops were getting cozy, she accidentally knocked his lunch on the floor, and he picked it up to brush it off. The woman said, "You're not going to eat it when it's that dirty, are you?"

"Say sandwich!" moaned Morales. "Say sandwich!"

Detective Gonzales, ace of the force, was talking to the chief. "I just can't get over how bold this murderer we're after is!"

"What do you mean?" asked his superior.

"Imagine," he said, "a guy murders someone, then he not only leaves his fingerprints on the knife in the guy's back but also his name and the year he was born."

"Are you sure?" said the chief.

"Certainly," replied the Mexican. "That's what it said on the weapon. Oneida, 1954."

* * *

Horace, a leading member of the San Francisco gay community, was on trial. He was charged with having oral sex with a plainclothes policeman, who arrested him afterward.

In court, the officer was asked to produce the evidence.

"I can't, Your Honor," cried the cop. "He swallowed it!"

* * *

A Nashville police car had been sent out of town on a false alarm. On the return trip, it passed Dural, a young black, leading two donkeys. The driver slowed down and said to the youngster, "Taking your brothers out for a walk, huh? But why are you holdin' the bridles so tight? Afraid they'll run away?"

"Yes, sir," said the boy. "I'm scared they'll run off and join the police force."

\* \* \*

Mercer and Orlando, two veteran patrolmen, were in the locker room dressing for duty.

"It was fantastic!" exclaimed Mercer to his partner. "Saturday night, I went to this big party, see, and pretty soon I noticed this great big blonde giving me the eye. We start talking, and all of a sudden she asks me to take her home. The minute we get into the car, she unzipped me and went right down—and I still don't even know her name."

"So what'd you do?" asked the other cop.

"Well, I figured this was one case where I'd shoot first and ask questions afterward."

\* \* \*

Patrol car 7 was cruising along New York's East River Drive when this radio message came in: "Calling car 19. Calling car 19. Go to Park Avenue and Thirty-seventh Street. Nude woman running down street. That is all."

Then the voice added, "All other cars remain on their beats."

## Lawbreaker Baubles

Judge Larson leaned over the bench and glared at the prisoner.

"How is it you can't get a lawyer to defend you?" he asked.

"As soon as they find out I didn't steal the money, they won't have anything to do with me."

* * *

"You have been convicted on nineteen counts, and you are hereby committed to the state prison with a cumulative sentence of ninety-nine years. Have you anything to offer?"

"Nothin', judge, except that you're pretty free with another man's time."

*　*　*

Gregarious Gary Cantor, the famous Fairfax Avenue restaurateur, tells about Ginsberg standing before a judge. "Have you anything to say before I pass sentence on you?"

"Yes, Your Honor. I think it would be nice you should have your lunch first."

*　*　*

"You've been acquitted on the charge of bigamy," said the judge. "You can go home to your wife now."

"Thank you, Your Honor," said the free man. "Which one?"

*　*　*

Fournier stood before the bar. The Frenchman was smartly attired, alert, and obviously intelligent.

"You have been charged with rape," said the magistrate. "How do you plead?"

"Not guilty by reason of insanity, Your Honor."

"Insanity?" exclaimed the judge.

"Yes, sir," said the defendant. "I'm just crazy about it."

*　*　*

# OVERHEARD IN DETROIT JAIL

*Lawyer:* O.K., Bussey, so you want me to defend you? Have you got any money?

*Bussey:* No, suh. I hain't got no money, but I got a 1978 Chrysler car.

*Lawyer:* Good, you can raise money on that. Now, let's see—just what do they accuse you of stealing?

*Bussey:* A 1978 Chrysler car.

\* \* \*

Kinsley had been accused of stealing a watch, but there was so little evidence the judge was forced to dismiss the case. The prisoner, however, just remained standing in the courtroom. "I said you're discharged," roared the magistrate. "You are acquitted. You're free. Get out."

"Excuse me, judge," said Kinsley, "but do that mean I gotta give the watch back?"

\* \* \*

Two city dwellers were discussing urban law-breakers.

"The holdups and robberies are really getting bad, aren't they?"

"Say, there's so much crime in my neighborhood, the intersection lights say, 'Shoot' and 'Don't Shoot'."

\* \* \*

Pinky the pickpocket went to visit a friend who had just been arrested.

"I had to hire a lawyer for you," he said, "and left my solid-gold watch for collateral."

"Did he keep it?"

"He thinks he did."

*   *   *

Did you hear about the convict serving a life sentence in a Massachusetts jail?

He writes a weekly column for the prison newspaper and calls it HERE TODAY, HERE TOMORROW.

*   *   *

Judge Meehan glared contemptuously at the tattered prisoner who had been dragged before him on a charge of vagrancy.

"Have you ever earned a dollar in your life?" he asked scornfully.

"Yes, Your Honor," was the response. "I voted for you at the last election."

*   *   *

"Do you mean to tell me that this man strangled a woman in a ballroom with over two hundred people present?"

"Yes, Your Honor. Everybody thought they were dancing."

*   *   *

"You've been convicted twenty-two times on this offense—aren't you ashamed to own up to that?"

"No, Your Honor. I don't think one ought to be ashamed of his convictions."

\* \* \*

*Magistrate:* This man's watch was fastened in his pocket by a safety pin. How did you manage to get it?
*Prisoner:* Well, judge, I usually gets $200 fer six lessons.

\* \* \*

Fred Manaster, the popular Los Angeles public defender, tells about the time a judge was ready to deliver a severe sentence. He looked at the defendant and said, "This robbery was consummated in an adroit and skillful manner."

"Come, now, Your Honor." The accused blushed. "No flattery, please."

\* \* \*

*Judge:* Have you anything to say, prisoner, before sentence is passed upon you?
*Prisoner:* No, Your Honor, except that it takes very little to please me.

\* \* \*

Comic Phil Leeds, the lovable lampooner, came up with this lulu:

Blackie and his partner climbed over the warehouse fence, broke a window, and entered the company office. After locating the safe, Blackie removed his shoes and socks. He wrapped his toe around the dials of the safe and began twirling them.

"Come on. Let's crack this crib and get outa here," said his pal. "Why fool around?"

"Ya gotta have a sense of humor," said Blackie. "Doin' it this way only takes a few minutes longer, and it drives those fingerprint experts nuts."

* * *

When Benny the burglar climbed out the window of the house, Wally, his waiting companion, asked, "What did you get?"

"It's a lawyer's home," said Benny.

"What did you lose?" asked Wally.

* * *

Before passing sentence, Judge Payton said to the pickpocket, "Just what good have you done for humanity?"

"Well," replied the crook, "I've kept three or four detectives working regularly."

* * *

Did you hear about the Baltimore woman who stabbed her husband 400 times?

She didn't know how to turn off the electic knife.

* * *

## BURGLAR

*A gent who is seeking an opening in the better mercantile establishments*

* * *

Roxanne was berating her boy friend. "You bum," she cried, "you even forgot what day this is."

"Aw," he said, "I didn't forget your birthday. I even went to da jewelry shop to get you somethin'—but he was still open."

* * *

Harry and Lester, two pickpockets, were talking shop.

"Say," jawed Harry, "where'd you get that lovely watch?"

"From my cousin," answered Lester.

"From which cousin?"

"How should I know? I found the watch, and on the cover it said, 'In memory of your grateful cousin.' "

* * *

Retired Sea Ranch CPA Jim Cockburn loves this silly Scots saga:

Jenkins and Billings, two robbers, held up an Edinburgh bank. They tied and gagged MacTavish, the cashier, and then herded the other employees into the vault. After they filled their sacks with loot and started to leave, MacTavish began thrashing about on the floor, making noises through the gag.

Jenkins loosened the gag and asked, "Whaddaya want?"

"Please!" whispered the Scotsman. "Take the books, too. I'm $26,000 shor-r-t!"

*   *   *

While walking through Central Park, a guy pointed a gun at Doran and said, "Stick 'em up and congratulations!"

"What's the congratulations for?" asked Doran.

"You are now entering a lower tax bracket," he replied.

*   *   *

Judge Kirkby was having dinner with Dr. Salisbury, the criminal psychologist, in a Minneapolis restaurant.

"It's strange," said the judge, "but I haven't had a pickpocket brought to the courtroom in months."

"That's not so strange," explained the psychologist. "Their season doesn't begin until May. Here in Minnesota people don't take their hands out of their pockets until then."

*   *   *

OVERHEARD IN CHICAGO LOOP

*Mugger:* This is a holdup! Give me your money or else.

*Victim:* Or else what?

*Mugger:* Don't confuse me. This is my first job.

*   *   *

*Burglar:* The police are coming! Quick, jump out the window!

*Accomplice:* But we're on the thirteenth floor!

*Burglar:* This is no time to be supersititious.

* * *

Rizzuti and his wife were sitting in their Brooklyn apartment when the police broke in and arrested him. He was charged with robbing a department store of two dozen dresses worth $19.95 each. The police found the cheap apparel and brought it to court as evidence.

"Did you steal these dresses?" asked the judge.

"Yeah," admitted Rizzuti.

"Before I sentence you," said the judge, "why did you take only the cheap $19.95 dresses when in the next rack were hundreds of very expensive gowns and furs?"

"Hey, judge, enough's enough!" said Rizzuti. "My wife's been buggin' me about it ever since I brought the damn dresses home!"

* * *

Joe Aucoin, the personable personal injury practitioner, cracks up clients with this cutie:

Miss Spratt the spinster thought she heard a noise, so she crept quietly down the stairs, not making a sound, walking on tiptoes. Just as she got to the last step, the housebreaker turned and saw her.

"Gee, lady," he remarked, "ain't you the quiet one comin' down those steps. You oughta be a burglar."

*  *  *

Did you hear about the flasher who wanted to quit but decided to stick it out a little longer?

*  *  *

"Have you a lawyer?" asked the judge.
"No, I don't need one," said the prisoner. "I got a lotta friends on the jury."

*  *  *

Marshall Morgan, the magnificent legal mastermind, makes colleagues merry with this snip of exaggeration:

Pete was found guilty, but before the judge passed sentence, his lawyer said, "Your Honor, I submit that my client did not break into the house. He found the living-room window open, inserted his right arm, and removed a few trifling articles. Now my client's arm is not himself, and I don't feel you should punish him for an offense committed by one of his limbs."

"Your argument," said the judge, "is very well put. However, I will follow your tenuous logic. I sentence the prisoner's right arm to one year's imprisonment. He can accompany the arm or not, as he chooses."

Whereupon the defendant calmly removed his artificial right arm, handed it to the speechless judge, and walked out of court with his lawyer.

The judge became exasperated when he saw the same woman before him on the same charges.

"Looking at your record," he said, "it appears that you have been before me and convicted forty-six times for petty stealing."

"That's about right, Your Honor," said the female heister. "None of us is perfect."

* * *

*Prisoner:* Judge, I don't know what to do.
*Judge:* Why, how's that?
*Prisoner:* I swore to tell the truth, but every time I try, some lawyer objects.

* * *

The warden felt sorry for Horace, one of his prisoners. It seems Horace never had visitors and stayed alone in his cell on visiting days.

"Horace," said the warden, "I notice you never have visitors. Don't you have any friends or family?"

"Oh, sure," replied Horace, "but they're all in here."

* * *

Ron Elkins, the top tinsel-town talent rep, relates this rib tickler:

In his East Side hideaway, Little Blinkey bowed his head and prayed. "Thank you, God, for our wonderful police and for putting in jail so many pickpockets, dirty crooks, and connivers. If it weren't for your divine help, Lord, my profession would be so overcrowded that a poor thief like me could never earn a decent living!"

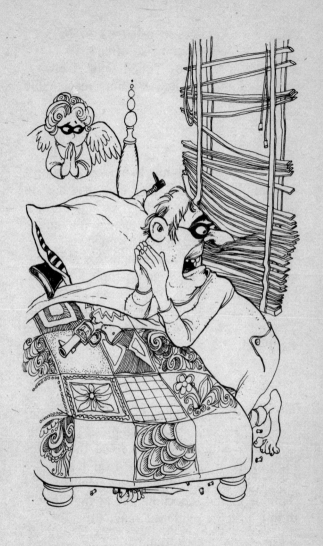

\* \* \*

**Judge:** Aren't you ashamed to be seen here in court so often?

**Prisoner:** Why, no, Your Honor. I always thought it was a very respectable place.

\* \* \*

There was so much evidence against Santini the swindler that the jury had to bring in a verdict of guilty.

After passing the sentence, the judge went into a harangue about con men.

"I think it is a reprehensible and contemptible thing to swindle people who have placed their trust in you," he said.

"But, Your Honor," said Santini, "people who don't trust you can't be swindled."

\* \* \*

Milner sashayed up to the bench. "Your Honor," he said, "I wanna plead guilty."

"Why didn't you do so at the beginning of the trial?" demanded the judge.

"Because," replied the accused, "I thought I was innocent, but at that time I didn't hear the evidence against me."

\* \* \*

\* \* \*

Willie, the gimp, was caught redhanded by a police officer as he was burglarizing a liquor store. At the trial, Judge Ward asked, "How do you plead?"

"Your Honor," answered the gimp, "before I plead guilty or not guilty, would the court please appoint a lawyer to defend me?"

"You were caught while committing the crime. What could any lawyer possibly say in your defense?"

"That's exactly my point, Your Honor," said Willie. "I'd like to hear what he could possibly say!"

\* \* \*

Did you hear about the convict who was going to the electric chair and called his lawyer for some last-minute advice?

The attorney said, "Don't sit down."

\* \* \*

A gentleman living in Phyffe
Made love to the corpse of his wife.
   He explained to the judge,
    "She was cold, didn't budge,
Just the same as she'd acted in life."

\* \* \*

Vincent Chieffo, the brainy Beverly Hills legal beagle, cheers chums with this chuckler:

One Sunday morning at a New Mexico prison, a group of inmates was being led to the Catholic and Protestant chapels. One prisoner did not enter either chapel but continued walking toward the main gate. A guard caught up with him and asked, "Where you going?"

The prisoner replied, "I was told I could go to the church of my choice, and it's in Dallas!"

* * *

*Judge:* So you claim you robbed that delicatessen store because you were starving? Why didn't you take something to eat instead of stealing all the cash out of the register?

*Evans:* 'Cause I'm a proud man, judge, an' I make it a rule to pay for everything I eat.

* * *

"How do you explain that this man's wallet was found in your pocket?" asked the judge.

"Your Honor," said the defendant, "life is a succession of inexplicable mysteries. I wish you would so instruct the jury."

* * *

In Arkansas, Levar was arrested and brought before Judge Whitney for having a still on his premises.

"How do you plead?" asked Whitney.

"I plead guilty and waive the hearing," said the black man.

"What do you mean 'waive the hearing'?" challenged the judge.

"I means I don't wanta heah no mo' about it."

* * *

In Hartford, a prosecuting attorney ordered the pretty defendant, "Tell the jury just why you shot your husband with a bow and arrow—"

"I didn't want to wake the children," said the woman.

\* \* \*

A white-haired black man was brought in from the mountains under suspicion of maintaining an illicit still. There was no real evidence against him.

"What's your name, prisoner?" asked the judge.

"Mah name's Joshua, jedge."

"Joshua, eh?" said the court. "Are you that same Joshua spoken of in Holy Writ— the Joshua who made the sun stand still?"

"No, jedge," he answered, " 'twan't me. Ah'm de Joshua dat made de moonshine still."

\* \* \*

*Judge:* I note that in addition to stealing money, you took watches, rings, and pearls.

*Prisoner:* Yes, Your Honor. I was taught that money alone does not bring happiness.

\* \* \*

In an Arkansas town, old Ozzie was charged with chicken stealing. "Where's your lawyer?" asked the magistrate.

"Ain't got none, jedge," replied the black man.

"But you ought to have one," returned the court. "I'll assign one to defend you."

"No, sah, please don't do dat," begged the defendant.

"Why not?" persisted the judge. "It won't cost you anything. Why don't you want a lawyer?"

"Well, Yo' Honor," said the old man, "Ah wants to enj'y dem chickens mahself."

\* \* \*

## Client Cracks

Ramsey's client was under arrest.

"You say you've a perfect answer to this wife murder charge," said the lawyer. "What is it?"

"She wasn't my wife."

* * *

"Now," said the lawyer, "are you sure you've told me all the truth? If I'm going to defend you, I've got to know everything."

"Yeah. I told yuh everything."

"Good. I think I can easily get you acquitted. You've got an excellent alibi that proves you're innocent, beyond a doubt, of this robbery. Now you are sure, absolutely sure, that you've told me everything?"

"Yeah. All except where I hid the money."

* * *

In Oklahoma, Riggs was accused of horse stealing. His lawyer saved him from conviction by a powerful plea. After his acquittal by the jury, the attorney took him aside and said, " 'Fess up, Rigg. You really stole that horse, didn't you?"

"Now, look a-here," was the reply, "I thought I stole that horse. But after yore speech to the jury, doggoned if I ain't got my doubts about it."

*　*　*

Mrs. Kibler suspected that her advertising executive husband was carrying on with his secretary.

She went to Durrett, an attorney, who specialized in marital problems. He put an investigator to work, and within a week Durrett discovered that the wife's suspicions were well founded. Mr. Kibler had his cute steno stashed in an East Side penthouse pad.

"I'll get him," said the wife. "How much would it cost to get concrete evidence enough to sue?"

"With one investigator, a photographer, and a witness," said the lawyer, "it will come to around $3,000."

"Get started right away!" snapped the woman. "I think I can borrow that much from my boy friend."

*　*　*

"Do you wish to challenge any of the jury?" asked the lawyer.

"Well," said his client, "I think I could lick that little guy on the end."

\* \* \*

*Lawyer:* When I was a boy, my ambition was to someday be a pirate.

*Client:* You're lucky. It's not every man who can have his dreams come true.

\* \* \*

Shapiro went to Birnbaum the attorney and told him that there would be no fee paid unless Birnbaum felt sure there were grounds for legal action.

Shapiro then gave the lawyer a detailed account of the trouble.

"My dear man, the case is airtight," shouted Birnbaum. "The other fellow hasn't got a leg to stand on. My advice is $100, and for another $300 retainer I'll start suit."

"No," said Shapiro, "you'd better not."

"But why?" demanded the lawyer.

" 'Cause," replied Shapiro, "I gave you the other fellow's side."

\* \* \*

"When the judge said he was releasin'
me in your custody, what did he mean?"

# OVERHEARD IN A SEVENTH AVE. RESTAURANT

*Nussbaum:* I'll sue you in the state court!

*Schrieber:* I'll meet you there!

*Nussbaum:* I'll sue you in the Supreme Court!

*Schrieber:* I'll be there to answer you!

*Nussbaum:* I'll sue you to the deepest level of hell!

*Schrieber:* My attorney'll be there!

\* \* \*

Rosenberg sat at the head table of his silver wedding anniversary party while his wife danced with one of the guests. Just then, Lieberman, his lawyer, stopped by to wish him well.

"Get away from me, you bum!" shouted Rosenberg.

"What's the matter?" asked the counselor. "I just want to congratulate you on being married twenty-five years."

"You should only drop dead!" exclaimed Rosenberg. "Some lawyer you are!"

"What are you talking about?"

"Don't you remember? After I was married ten years, I decided I had enough and I was gonna kill my wife. You told me not to do it, that I would get fifteen years in prison."

"So?" asked the attorney. "Why are you angry?"

"Because if I didn't listen to your advice, today I would be a free man!"

* * *

Goldstone and Sanford, two dress manufacturers, had a big argument. Goldstone consulted a lawyer about dividing the business so that he could buy Sanford out.

After several days, the attorney reported to his client: "I've finally talked your partner into seeing things your way, and he has agreed to a settlement that is very fair to both of you."

"Fair to both of us!" exclaimed Goldstone. "I could've done that myself. What'd I hire a lawyer for?"

* * *

Aunt Millie, a spinster, told the young lawyer who was making out her will that she had $5,000. Half was to go for her burial expenses and the other half to him if he would spend the night with her so she would not have to die a virgin.

Three days later, when the lawyer had not come home, his wife rushed over to the old maid's house. "Is my husband here?" she demanded.

"Yes, dearie! I've decided to let the town bury me!"

* * *

Mrs. Walker just got a third divorce and was celebrating at dinner with her attorney. "This might be hard for you to accept," said the happy divorcée, "but even though I've been married three times, I'm still a virgin."

"That's practically impossible," exclaimed the lawyer. "How could you possibly be a virgin after being married three times?"

"Well, my first husband was a salesman, and all he wanted to do was talk to it! My second spouse was an optician, and all he would do was look at it. And my third husband was a restaurant critic."

* * *

Dennis, a twelve-year-old boy who was accused of fathering a child, stood before the judge. The attorney, in order to prove the ridiculousness of the charge, unzipped the youngster's pants.

"Your Honor," said the lawyer, "look at this tiny organ, this immature equipment. How could a boy father a baby with this little, undeveloped—"

"Hey, mister," whispered the boy, "you better quit stroking me like that or we're gonna lose this case!"

Dale Williamson, the brilliant Coldwell Banker veep, beams over this nifty nugget:

Landesman was coming down the street on crutches.

"What in the world happened to you?" asked his friend Kirkland.

"Got hit by a bus a couple of months ago," said Landesman.

"Two months ago?" asked Kirkland. "And you still aren't able to walk without crutches?"

"Well," said the man, "my doctor says I can walk without them, but my lawyer thinks I should keep using them for a while."

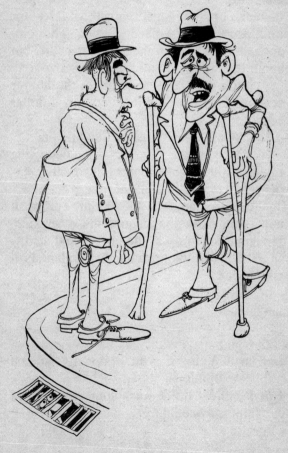

*   *   *

Percy Rodrigues, the talented television star, teases attorney pals with this titillator:

Sciola was walking along a Detroit street when he fell through an open sewer hole and broke his leg. He hired a prominent lawyer, brought suit against the city for $300,000, and won the case. The city appealed the case to the supreme court, but again the attorney won the decision.

After the claim was settled, the lawyer sent for his client and handed him a dollar bill.

"What's this?" asked Sciola.

"That's your damages after deducting my fee, the cost of appeal, and other expenses," replied the attorney.

Sciola stared at the dollar, turned it over, and carefully scanned the other side. He then looked up at the lawyer and said:

"What's wrong with this dollar? Is it counterfeit?"

*   *   *

*Lawyer:* Well, if you want my honest opinion—

*Client:* No, no. I want your professional advice.

*   *   *

Bonniwell sat with a group of farmers in a small country store. "I sure hate to hear you lambasting them lawyers the way you been doin'," said Bonniwell. "Last year, a lawyer made me a present of $200."

"Come off!"

"Yes, he did!"

"What are you givin' us?"

"It's the Gospel truth," he said. "I was injured in a railroad accident last year, and this lawyer sued the railroad company and got $10,000 damages. His bill was $10,200, but he didn't say a word about the $200 balance. He made me a present of it."

\* \* \*

Marlene rushed into Bigham's office. "I want him arrested! He threw me on the bed. He—oh, it was awful!"

"Now calm down," said the attorney. "Let's hear the whole story. What did he do first!"

"He locked the door!"

"Aha, kidnapping!" said Bigham, writing on a pad. "Ten years. Then what did he do?"

"He pulled up my skirt."

"Indecent exposure. Two more years." He made a note. "Then what?"

"He put his hand on my—my—"

"I understand—attempted assault. Five years. And then what?"

"He threw me on the bed."

"Ah, hah! Mayhem and felonious constraint. Ten to fifteen years. And then?"

"Then—he did it to me!"

"That's Rape! Thirty years—maybe we can get him the gas chamber. And meanwhile you were screaming and struggling—"

"Well-l-l-l, not exactly. It was kind of late, and I didn't want to disturb everybody, and—"

"Ah, nuts!" cried the lawyer, tearing up his notes, "that's just a plain ordinary screw!"

* * *

## *Mouthpiece Monkeyshines*

The lawyer was down and out. "How's business?" asked a contemporary.

"I just got eviction papers," he said sadly. "Wrote them up myself. Wouldn't have done it if I didn't need the money."

\* \* \*

Chaffin had just won his first case, and the client, a man acquitted of a burglary charge, came over to congratulate him.

"Thanks a lot," said the felon. "I'll drop in on you sometime."

"Fine," said the lawyer. "All I ask is that you make it in the daytime."

\* \* \*

Honorable Bernard Gross, the former municipal court magistrate, related this wacky winner:

"Your Honor," said Bennett, "my client has a small case in this court, and we are not prepared to go on with it this morning. I'd like to have a two-week adjournment?"

"Why?" asked Judge Landon.

"My client is out of town, training for a prize fight."

"Frankly," said the judge, "that reason does not interest me."

"But," said the lawyer, "it interests me. He's fighting for my fee."

\* \* \*

Hagen was carrying a load of books into court. His client said, "I thought you carried all the law in your head?"

"I do," replied the lawyer. "These books are for the judge."

\* \* \*

In Norway, country of the midnight sun, a sensational trial was in progress. The prosecuting attorney shook his fist in the face of the accused and thundered, "I ask you again, sir, where were you on the night of October thirtieth to April first?"

\* \* \*

The blonde on the witness stand looked like a movie starlet. The attorney smiled at her and asked, "Where were you, my dear, night before last?"

"Entertaining a gentleman friend," she replied.

"And where were you last night?" he persisted.

"Entertaining another gentleman friend," she admitted.

"And where are you going to be tonight?" whispered the judge.

"Objection!" shouted the prosecuting attorney. "I asked her first!"

\* \* \*

Dr. Bradford telephoned his lawyer to discuss a malpractice insurance problem. "It's a big headache," said Bradford.

"I know," said the lawyer, "but it's late. Why don't you take two aspirin and call me in the morning?"

\* \* \*

A Hollywood lawyer is building a big reputation in the movie colony because of his success in handling delicate cases. His latest one involved a prominent motion-picture actor who was arrested on charges of sodomy.

The lawyer got the charge reduced to tailgating.

Klippert flew to California to try an important case, promising to wire his partner the moment a decision was announced. At long last, the wire came:

JUSTICE HAS TRIUMPHED

The partner in New York wired back:

APPEAL AT ONCE

* * *

Harry Palmer, Farmer's best loved insurance rep, finds fun in this little lulu:

Dr. Gavin and Allison, an attorney, were driving in separate autos along the California Coast Highway one foggy night. The cars collided, but the fault was questionable. Both men were shaken up, and the lawyer offered the doctor some whiskey from a pocket flask.

Gavin took the flask with a shaking hand and took several long swallows. When Allison started to cap the flask, the doctor said, "A stiff drink could help the nerves. Why don't you have one, also?"

"Oh, I will," replied the lawyer, "right after the highway patrol gets here."

* * *

Doctor Patterson was fuming when he finally reached his table at a charity dinner. Patterson explained to the lawyer seated next to him that a woman he'd just met kept badgering him for advice on a personal medical problem.

"I'd like to send her a bill," declared the doctor.

"Of course," replied the lawyer. "You rendered professional services even if only informally."

"Thanks," said Patterson, "I'll just do that."

The next day, the doctor went to his office, prepared to send the annoying woman a bill. On his desk, he found a letter from the lawyer: "For legal services, $100."

* * *

## PHYSICIANS' PHILOSOPHY

*Some doctors direct their patients to lie always on the right side, declaring that it is injurious to the health to lie on both sides. Yet lawyers as a class enjoy good health.*

* * *

Carlson, an elderly miser, lay on his deathbed. He had no friends, so he summoned his doctor, lawyer, and minister to his bedside. "They say you can't take it with you, but I am going to prove you can," gasped the dying man. "I've got $300,000 in cash under my mattress. It's in three envelopes of $100,000 each. I want you each to take an envelope now, and just before they shovel the dirt on me, you throw the envelopes in."

The three attended the funeral, and each threw in his envelope. On the way back from the cemetery, the minister said, "Gentlemen, I want to confess. I needed $30,000 badly for a new church building, so I took out $30,000 and threw only $70,000 in the grave."

"I gotta tell the truth, too!" said the doctor. "I'm building a hospital and took $50,000 and threw in only $50,000."

"Fellas," said the lawyer, "I'm shocked. Keeping that money was a shameful thing to do. I threw in my personal check for the full amount."

* * *


A lawyer and a doctor were arguing about the relative merits of their professions.

"I don't say," said the doctor, "that all lawyers are thieves. But you'll have to admit that your profession does not make angels of men."

"You're right," answered the lawyer. "We leave that up to you doctors."


* * *


Jackson needed legal advice, and so he walked into the office of Larker, Newly, and Larker. The black man sat down at the desk of the senior member of the firm.

"If you're not really in bad trouble, I'll take the case," said Larker. "If you're in a jam and want to get out of it, my partner will handle it. If, on the other hand, you're not involved and want to get in trouble, my son, who just graduated from law school, will take it!"


* * *

Berkowitz had just opened his Miami Beach law office. He immediately hired three sun-kissed blonde stenographers, each more bosomy than the other, to work for him.

A friend stopped by the office, and after eyeballing the three beauties, asked, "How the devil do you expect to accomplish anything?"

"Easy," replied Berkowitz. "I'll give two of them the day off."

* * *

Fowler was sitting in his Portland office, smoking a cigar. There was a knock at the door, and the secretary ushered in Roberts, a new client.

"What can I do for you?" asked the lawyer.

"I think I'm gonna be in a paternity suit."

"Why?"

"I've fathered nineteen children," replied Roberts.

"Nineteen!" exclaimed Fowler. "How come you have so many kids?"

"I just love to make love."

"I love my cigar, too, but I take it out once in a while."

* * *

Helga Noice, the curvy cruise ship hostess, gets howls with this hunk of hyperbole:

Thatcher graduated from law school and was taken into his father's firm. "Any advice, dad," he asked.

"Yes, my boy, when fighting a case, it's always been my policy that if the law is on my side, I hammer on the law. If the facts are on my side, I hammer on the facts."

"But if you don't have the facts or the law?" asked Thatcher.

"In that case, I hammer on the table."

\* \* \*

Byrke, in a state of hysteria, went to an attorney. "What am I going to do?" he asked. "McLaughlin is suing me for breaking an irreplaceable antique plate of his!"

"Don't worry," said the lawyer. "We have at least three lines of defense. In the first place, we will prove that you never borrowed the plate from McLaughlin. In the second place, we'll prove that when you borrowed the plate, it was already damaged beyond repair. And in the third place, we'll prove that when you returned it, it was in absolutely perfect condition."

\* \* \*

One morning before court proceedings in Seattle, Judge Trindle joked with a young lawyer. "If you and I were turned into a horse and an ass, which would you prefer to be?"

"The horse," replied the counselor. "I've heard of an ass being made a judge, but a horse never."

*   *   *

Dietz and Beaumont, two Park Avenue lawyers, were taking a shower together at the New York Athletic Club. "Hey," said Dietz, "how'd you get such a big dong?"

"When I was a kid in the Bronx," replied Beaumont, "we were so poor I didn't have any toys to play with."

*   *   *

A Chicago woman in desperate trouble persuaded the great Clarence Darrow to handle her litigation. The lawyer defended her brilliantly and won her case in a breeze.

When it was all over, she said to him, "Oh, Mr. Darrow, how can I ever show my appreciation?"

"My dear woman," responded Darrow, "ever since the Phoenicians invented money, there has been only one answer to that question."

*   *   *

Coleman checked into a Manhattan hotel and said to the desk clerk, "Would you put this $500 in the safe?" The next morning, when Coleman called for his cash, the clerk said, "I don't know about any money. Have you got a receipt?"

"No," said the guest, "but I gave you five hundred-dollar bills for safekeeping, and you put them in an envelope."

"I'm sorry. You're mistaken."

Coleman consulted a Park Avenue lawyer. "Tell you what to do," he advised. "Give that clerk another $500 but do it in front of a friend. Return an hour later without your friend and ask for your cash. The clerk will return your money this time because you have a witness. Two hours later, go back with your friend and tell the clerk, 'I'd like to have the money I left with you while my friend was here.' The clerk'll feel trapped and give you back the first five hundred bucks."

Coleman did as he was advised, and it worked. He returned to the lawyer and praised him for his shrewdness.

"Now what is your fee?" he asked.

"Five hundred dollars."

Langford sat in an attorney's office and in hushed tones confessed, "I stole $10,000 from the bank I work at. What'll I do?"

"Steal $5,000 more and bring it to me," advised the lawyer.

Langford did as he was told and brought the cash to him. The lawyer wrote the following letter, which got Langford off.

*Gentlemen:*

*Your cashier took $15,000 from your bank. The hard-pressed family, despite the most desperate efforts, was unable to raise more than $5,000, which they offer if you will not prosecute.*

\* \* \*

Anderson had only been practicing for two years and was barely eking out a living. His wife nagged him constantly about their modest home furnishings.

"We need a new dining-room set," she complained. "We need a new rug in the living room. We need a new television set. We need—"

"Okay," interrupted the young lawyer. "Soon you'll have all the new furniture you want."

"Why, what happened?"

"A wealthy client came to the office today. He's suing his wife for divorce. Now just as soon as I break up his home, you can furnish ours!"

Bobby Ramsen, the consummate comedic thespian, snickers over this satirical saga:

A lawyer attended the funeral of a rich man. A friend, arriving late, took a seat beside him and whispered, "How far has the service gone?"

The lawyer nodded toward the clergyman in the pulpit and whispered back, "He just opened for the defense."

Peter Alpert, the jolly jogging West Coast real estate attorney, tells this wonderful wisp of waggery:

Young Baylock had just moved into his new San Francisco office and was awaiting his first client. Suddenly, footsteps were coming down the hall, heading for his office. Quickly, the new bar member sat down behind his desk, picked up the phone, and began talking to nobody.

"Well," said Baylock, "I'm very busy right now, and I've got to be in court this afternoon and again tomorrow morning. Then I have an appointment with clients all tomorrow afternoon and the next day."

He looked up to see a man standing at the door watching, then continued his make-believe conversation to make certain he impressed the man.

"Perhaps," he said into the phone, "I can squeeze you in Thursday afternoon. Good. See you then."

Baylock hung up the phone and turned to the man at the door. "Yes, can I be of some help?"

"No," he replied, "I just came to connect your telephone."

The courtroom was packed. Attorney Collins raised his voice so everyone could hear plainly.

"Repeat the words the defendant used," said the lawyer.

"I'd rather not. They were not fit words to tell a gentleman."

"Then," said the attorney, "whisper them to the judge."

\* \* \*

In Atlanta, Bloom the butcher burst open the door marked *Private* and stood before Ames the attorney.

"If a dog steals a piece of meat from my shop, is the owner liable?" he asked.

"Certainly," replied the lawyer.

"Okay, your dog took a piece of sirloin steak worth $10 about five minutes ago."

"That right?" said Ames. "Then just give me another $10, and that'll cover my fee."

\* \* \*

Child psychologists claim children are strongly affected by the kind of work done by the male parent. Guess what this youngster's dad does for a living:

"Mark, did you take that candy? Answer me this instant!"

"What candy?"

"You know very well what candy. Did you take it?"

"That's a leading question. I can't incriminate myself."

"Mark!"

"And besides, it's no crime to take candy because there's no mention of candy in the Constitution."

"Mark, I'm losing patience. Once more, did you take that candy?"

"I'd like a delay until next fall to prepare my case. My witnesses have gone to Mexico!"

"You're overruled. If I waited, you might destroy the evidence."

"Then I want a change of venue."

"Overruled. This is just as good a place as a woodshed."

"Can I have a habeas corpus?"

"Mark, you're hurting your own case by all this quibbling. Come on now. Did you take it, or didn't you?"

"I'd like to appeal the case to some court that isn't in session."

"Nonsense. This court is capable of trying it. If you're guilty, I want to know it; and if you're innocent, I should think you'd be glad to have a chance to prove it. Are you guilty or not guilty?"

"Not guilty!"

*  *  *

\* \* \*

Miss Drantz heard one of her pupils crying and rushed out to the playground.

"What is the trouble?" she asked of little Paul, who was eating an apple.

"Alvin took Ken's apple," explained the witness.

"And where is the apple?" asked the teacher.

"I've got that," replied Paul. "You see, I'm the lawyer."

\* \* \*

A potential client asked the lawyer, "And what is a contingent fee?"

"A contingent fee to a lawyer means if I don't win your suit, I get nothing. If I do win it, you get nothing."

\* \* \*

*Client:* I know the evidence is strongly against my innocence, but I have $50,000 to fight the case.

*Lawyer:* As your attorney, I assure you that you'll never go to prison with that amount of money.

And he didn't. He went in broke.

\* \* \*

Phillips was cross-examining a reluctant witness, "Is it true, miss, that you are a prostitute?"

"That's my business," was the indignant reply.

"I see," said the lawyer. "Then would you please tell the court your hobbies."

\* \* \*

If you were to give someone a tangerine, you'd simply say, "I give you this tangerine!"

But when the transaction is turned over to a legal practitioner, this is the way he puts it down:

*I hearby give and convey to you all and singular, my estate and interests, rights, title, claim, and advantages of and in said tangerine, together with all its rind, juice, pulp, and pits and all rights and advantages with full power to bite, cut, and otherwise eat the same or give the same away with and without the rind, skin, juice, pulp, or pits, anything herein before or herein after or in any other deed or deeds, instruments of whatever nature or kind whatsoever to the contrary in anywise notwithstanding.*

Then a couple of smart Philadelphia lawyers come along and take it away from you.

\* \* \*

* * *

Foster and Williams, the senior partners in the firm of Foster, Williams, Mason, Manning, Nevins, Rieger, and Block, were having a heated argument over the subject of sex.

"I believe," announced Foster, "that sex is 90 percent work and 10 percent fun."

"Ridiculous," shouted Williams. "Sex is 10 percent work and 90 percent fun."

Just then, Lawson, their young law clerk, entered the room. The partners agreed to let him settle the argument.

When asked his opinion, Lawson said, "Far as I'm concerned, it's 100 percent fun."

"How do you figure that?" bellowed Williams.

"It's simple," said the clerk. "If there was any work to it, you gentlemen would have me doing it for you!"

* * *

Monsieur Le Grand, a leading solicitor from Paris, was visiting friends in Boston. At a dinner party, a Massachusetts lawyer said, smiling, "All French law cases are always about sex!"

"That's not true, Monsieur," said the Frenchman. "Take the case I'm handling now. It's simply a family problem. My client, Jean Louis, was in love with Nanette, but she was afraid of losing her virginity and made him promise he wouldn't penetrate her maidenhead.

"Jean Louis did exactly as he promised, but just at that special moment, Nanette's mother burst into the bedroom, saw what was going on, became furiously angry, and gave Jean Louis a tremendous kick in the behind.

"He relieved himself, the girl got pregnant, and my client claims that the girl's mother is the father of the child!"

\* \* \*

The defense attorney neared the end of summation.

"Gentlemen of the jury," he said, getting warmed up, "the real question here before you is, Shall this beautiful young widow be forced to languish away her best years in a dark prison cell? Or shall she be set free to return to her charming little apartment at 437 East Eighty-second Street, there to spend her lonely, loveless hours in her boudoir, lying beside her tiny touch-tone phone, 465-8237?"

\* \* \*

Barbara and Alan, a young law clerk, were in court observing an indecent-exposure case. Suddenly, the defendant jumped up during cross-examination, pulled down his trousers and shorts, and began masturbating.

"Isn't that illegal?" gasped the girl.

"Sure as hell is," answered the fledgling attorney. "Why, he's getting fingerprints all over exhibit A!"

\* \* \*

## *Lien Lines*

Each profession has its oft-told list of humorous bromides. These legal beagle barbs survive the test of time because they hit the proverbial nail on the head. Here are some classics on members of the Bar:

Ignorance of the law is no excuse unless you can afford to hire a good lawyer.

\* \* \*

Possession is nine points of the law, and lawyers' fees are the other ninety-one points.

\* \* \*

\* \* \*

Ignorance of the law does not prevent the losing lawyer from collecting his bill.

\* \* \*

A lawyer is a man who prevents someone else from getting your money.

\* \* \*

Talk is cheap—if lawyers don't do the talking.

\* \* \*

Only lawyers can write documents containing five thousand or more words and call it a brief.

\* \* \*

A client between two lawyers is like a fish between two cats.

\* \* \*

If you can't get a lawyer who knows the law, get one who knows the judge.

\* \* \*

* * *

After they become judges, they stop practicing law.

* * *

Some lawyers think the art of cross-examination is to examine crossly.

* * *

An attorney is like a porcupine. It's impossible to touch him without pricking one's finger.

* * *

A lawyer is an expert on justice as a prostitute is an expert on love.

* * *

An attorney rescues your estate from your enemies so that he may keep it himself.

* * *

Where there's a will, there's a delay.

* * *

There are now over 40 million laws to enforce the Ten Commandments.

You can easily detect a lawyer who settles wills—he grins from heir to heir.

* * *

He who would travel from law to logic must jump many fences.

* * *

Lawyers sometimes tell the truth—they will do anything to win a case.

* * *

Ignorance of the law excuses no man—from practicing it.

* * *

There are two kinds of lawyers; those who know the law and those who know the judge.

* * *

A lawyer is a man who gets two people to strip for a fight and then runs off with their clothes.

* * *

*   *   *

A lawyer is a guy who represents you just to make sure you get all that's coming to him.

*   *   *

It takes a lot of suits to keep a lawyer well dressed.

*   *   *

When an irresistible force meets an immovable body, there's usually a lawyer who will take the case.

*   *   *

Folks down South say that if there is one lawyer in town, he's poor—if there are two lawyers in town, both are rich.

*   *   *

Find a Jewish boy who doesn't go to medical school and you'll find a lawyer.

*   *   *

The reason there are so few women lawyers is because women would rather lay down the law than take it up.

\* \* \*

The law is a system that protects every-body who can afford to hire a good lawyer.

\* \* \*

The law is supposed to speak for itself—if it did, it would complain against lawyers.

\* \* \*

A lawyer is the only person in whom ignorance of the law is not punished.

\* \* \*

A Texas lawyer got his client a sus-pended sentence. They hung him.

\* \* \*

The average man thinks lawyers are dishonest because if he were a lawyer, he would be dishonest.

\* \* \*

There are only two kinds of women clients—those who pay liberally and those who complain to the Bar Association.

\* \* \*

One thing all lawyers agree on: Be nice to everybody. You never know who may show up on the jury.

* * *

Something else members of the bar will tell you:
It is sad to see people squandering money and know you cannot help them.

* * *

In the United States, Congress makes the laws, the Supreme Court interprets them, the president executes them, and the citizens disobey them.

* * *

188

## ABOUT THE AUTHOR

LARRY WILDE, the world's best-known jokesmith, was born in Jersey City, spent two years in the U.S. Marine Corps, and then graduated from the University of Miami, Florida, with a Bachelor of Arts degree. He started his career in show business as a stand-up comedian, playing the nation's nightclubs and theaters and appearing on television commercials and sitcoms. Mr. Wilde's twenty-four books (which include two comprehensive studies on the serious business of comedy, *The Great Comedians* and *How the Great Comedy Writers Create Laughter*) are now read in every English-speaking land as well as in six other foreign countries. With sales of over 6 million his "Official" joke books have become the largest selling humor series in the history of publishing. Larry Wilde, who has been making America laugh for more than 25 years, is married to a former Wyoming beauty queen. Mrs. Wilde has just published her first book, *The Best of Ethnic Home Cooking*. The Wildes reside in Los Angeles.

## BOOKS BY LARRY WILDE

THE OFFICIAL BEDROOM/BATHROOM JOKE
  BOOK
*More* THE OFFICIAL DEMOCRAT/REPUBLICAN
  JOKE BOOK
*More* THE OFFICIAL SMART KIDS/DUMB PARENTS
  JOKE BOOK
THE OFFICIAL BOOK OF SICK JOKES
*More* THE OFFICIAL JEWISH/IRISH JOKE BOOK
THE *Last* OFFICIAL ITALIAN JOKE BOOK
THE OFFICIAL CAT LOVERS/DOG LOVERS JOKE
  BOOK
THE OFFICIAL DIRTY JOKE BOOK
THE *Last* OFFICIAL POLISH JOKE BOOK
THE OFFICIAL GOLFERS JOKE BOOK
THE OFFICIAL SMART KIDS/DUMB PARENTS
  JOKE BOOK
THE OFFICIAL RELIGIOUS/*Not So* RELIGIOUS JOKE
  BOOK
THE OFFICIAL DEMOCRAT/REPUBLICAN JOKE
  BOOK
*More* THE OFFICIAL POLISH/ITALIAN JOKE BOOK
THE OFFICIAL BLACK FOLKS/WHITE FOLKS JOKE
  BOOK
THE OFFICIAL VIRGINS/SEX MANIACS JOKE
  BOOK
THE OFFICIAL JEWISH/IRISH JOKE BOOK
THE OFFICIAL POLISH/ITALIAN JOKE BOOK

and

THE COMPLETE BOOK OF ETHNIC HUMOR
  (Pinnacle)
HOW THE GREAT COMEDY WRITERS CREATE
  LAUGHTER (Nelson-Hall)
THE GREAT COMEDIANS (Citadel Press)